双双中文教材 (20)
Chinese Language and Culture Course

中国历史（下）History of China (II)

王双双 编著

北京大学出版社
PEKING UNIVERSITY PRESS

图书在版编目（CIP）数据

中国历史.下/王双双 编著.—北京：北京大学出版社，2007.11
（双双中文教材20）
ISBN 978-7-301-08705-3

Ⅰ.中… Ⅱ.王… Ⅲ.汉语–对外汉语教学–教材 Ⅳ.H195.4

中国版本图书馆CIP数据核字（2005）第075456号

书　　　　名：	中国历史（下）
著 作 责 任 者：	王双双　编著
英 文 翻 译：	王亦兵
责 任 编 辑：	孙　娴
标 准 书 号：	ISBN 978-7-301-08705-3/ H·1441
出 版 发 行：	北京大学出版社
地　　　　址：	北京市海淀区成府路205号　100871
网　　　　址：	http://www.pup.cn
电　　　　话：	邮购部 62752015　发行部 62750672　编辑部 62752028　出版部 62754962
电 子 信 箱：	zpup@pup.pku.edu.cn
印 刷 者：	三河市博文印刷有限公司
经 销 者：	新华书店
	889毫米×1194毫米　16开本　10.75印张　163千字
	2007年11月第1版　2021年11月第5次印刷
定　　　价：	88.00元（含课本、练习册和CD-ROM盘一张）

未经许可，不得以任何方式复制或抄袭本书之部分或全部内容。
版权所有，侵权必究
举报电话：（010）62752024
电子信箱：fd@pup.pku.edu.cn

前言

《双双中文教材》是一套专门为海外青少年编写的中文课本，是我在美国八年的中文教学实践基础上编写成的。在介绍这套教材之前，请读一首小诗：

> 一双神奇的手，
> 推开一扇窗。
> 一条神奇的路，
> 通向灿烂的中华文化。
>
> 鲍凯文 鲍维江
> 1998年

鲍维江和鲍凯文姐弟俩是美国生美国长的孩子，也是我的学生。1998年冬，他们送给我的新年贺卡上的小诗，深深地打动了我的心。我把这首诗看成我文化教学的"回声"。我要传达给海外每位中文老师：我教给他们（学生）中国文化，他们思考了、接受了、回应了。这条路走通了！

语言是交际的工具，更是一种文化和一种生活方式，所以学习中文也就离不开中华文化的学习。汉字是一种古老的象形文字，她从远古走来，带有大量的文化信息，但学起来并不容易。使学生增强兴趣、减小难度，走出苦学汉字的怪圈，走进领悟中华文化的花园，是我编写这套教材的初衷。

学生不论大小，天生都有求知的欲望，都有欣赏文化美的追求。中华文化本身是魅力十足的。把这宏大而玄妙的文化，深入浅出地，有声有色地介绍出来，让这迷人的文化如涓涓细流，一点一滴地渗入学生们的心田，使学生们逐步体味中国文化，是我编写这套教材的目的。

为此我将汉字的学习放入文化介绍的流程之中同步进行，让同学们在学中国地理的同时，学习汉字；在学中国历史的同时，学习汉字；在学中国哲学的同时，学习汉字；在学中国科普文选的同时，学习汉字……

这样的一种中文学习，知识性强，趣味性强；老师易教，学生易学。当学生们合上书本时，他们的眼前是中国的大好河山，是中国五千年的历史和妙不可言的哲学思维，是奔腾的现代中国……

总之，他们了解了中华文化，就会探索这片土地，热爱这片土地，就会与中国结下情缘。

最后我要衷心地感谢所有热情支持和帮助我编写教材的老师、家长、学生、朋友和家人，特别是老同学唐玲教授、何茜老师、我姐姐王欣欣编审和她的儿子杨眉及我女儿Uta Guo年复一年的鼎力相助。可以说这套教材是大家努力的结果。

王双双
2005年5月8日

说明

《双双中文教材》是一套专门为海外学生编写的中文教材。它是由美国加州王双双老师和中国专家学者共同努力，在海外多年的实践中编写出来的。全书共 20 册，识字量 2500 个，包括了从识字、拼音、句型、短文的学习，到初步的较系统的中国文化的学习。教材大体介绍了中国地理、历史、哲学等方面的丰富内容，突出了中国文化的魅力。课本知识面广，趣味性强，深入浅出，易教易学。

这套教材体系完整、构架灵活、使用面广。学生可以从零起点开始，一直学完全部课程 20 册；也可以将后 11 册（10～20 册）的九个文化专题和第五册（汉语拼音）单独使用，这样便于高中和大学开设中国哲学、地理、历史等专门课程以及假期班、短期中国文化班、拼音速成班使用，符合美国 AP 中文课程的目标和基本要求。

本书是《双双中文教材》的第二十册，由王双双在杨东梁先生（中国人民大学图书馆馆长、清史研究所所长）的指导和帮助之下，在海外中文教学实践的基础上编写而成。全书语言简单，概要地介绍了中国从唐代下半叶到清代末期的历史知识。学生们通过学习，不仅能较系统地了解中国历史，中文的识字数量和语汇水平也将得到明显的提高。

考虑到海外汉语历史教学的特殊性，为了便利教学，本书的编写采取了化繁为简的原则，历史年代表中没有以王朝兴起的年代为它的起始年代，而是以它正式替代前朝的时间为准，如：秦、清等朝；或者以正式设立本国号的年代为准，如：辽、元等朝。特此说明。

编者

课程设置

一年级	中文课本(第一册)	中文课本(第二册)	中文课本(第三册)
二年级	中文课本(第四册)	中文课本(第五册)	中文课本(第六册)
三年级	中文课本(第七册)	中文课本(第八册)	中文课本(第九册)
四年级	中国成语故事	中国地理常识	
五年级	中国古代故事	中国神话传说	
六年级	中国古代科学技术	中国文学欣赏	
七年级	中国诗歌欣赏	中文科普阅读	
八年级	中国古代哲学	中国历史(上)	
九年级	中国历史(下)	小说阅读，中文SAT II	
十年级	中文SAT II (强化班)	小说阅读，中文SAT II 考试	

目录

第十一课	唐（下）	1
第十二课	五代十国和北宋	13
第十三课	辽、西夏、金与南宋	25
第十四课	成吉思汗和他的子孙	37
第十五课	元	45
第十六课	明（上）	57
第十七课	明（下）	69
第十八课	清（上）	78
第十九课	清（下）	88
生字表		99
生词表		101
中国历史朝代年表		105

第十一课

唐（下）

唐朝建立之后，一直蓬勃发展。从唐太宗到唐玄宗统治前期的一百多年间是唐朝的全盛时期。这时的唐朝政治安定，经济繁荣，文化发达，军力强大，是当时世界上最富庶、强盛的国家。

安史之乱

唐玄宗统治后期，生活奢侈，皇宫里专门织锦、刺绣的工匠就有700人。唐玄宗宠爱杨贵妃，不再关心国家的事情。他任用杨贵妃的堂兄杨国忠为宰相，国家混乱、腐败。

公元755年，军阀安禄山与部将史思明起兵反唐，占领长安，史称"安史之乱"。唐玄宗仓皇逃往四川。走到半路，愤怒的将士们杀死了杨国忠，并要求皇帝把杨贵妃处死。唐玄宗无奈，只好让人处死了杨贵妃。

唐代贵族铜镜（镶黄金飞鸟和白银花朵）

后来太子继帝位，史称唐肃宗。唐军经过八年战斗，最后平定了叛乱。安史之乱使人民无家可归，田地荒芜，唐朝从此由强盛走向衰落。

唐中期以后，均田制被破坏，许多大官占有良田万亩，而失地的农民越来越多，他们生活日益困苦，不断起来反抗。

唐朝末年爆发了黄巢起义，义军兵力达10余万人。起义军转战大半个中国，最后攻占了长安，黄巢称帝，国号"大齐"。但是起义军将领朱温叛变，黄巢被唐军打败，退出长安，后来在泰山附近兵败自杀。

黄巢起义失败后，各地军队将领的势力更大。公元907年，武将朱温政变成功，建立梁朝，建国290年的唐帝国灭亡。

灿烂的隋唐文化

隋唐时期，是中国经济文化繁荣开放的时期。隋唐政府积极同各国交往，当时与中国通商的国家有70多个。长安不仅是唐朝的首都，也是当时世界的一个中心。来自新罗（朝鲜）、日本、波斯和东罗马等国的几千名外国商人和留学生云集在长安、洛阳、广州等城市。唐朝政府平等对待他们，允许他们长期在中国居住，和中国

乐舞壁画（唐）

第十一课

波斯人物白玉带板（唐）

人通婚甚至在中国当官。在长安、洛阳这些大城市，有许多外国商人开的商店和酒馆，其中西域商人开的商店最多。在那里，人们可以吃到胡人①的美味食品，欣赏胡人的优美乐舞。唐代胡人多彩的服饰也深受汉族妇女的喜爱。

那时，朝鲜音乐也受到中国人的广泛欢迎。这一时期，汉族有机会和其他民族生活在一起，各族文化相互交流，使汉族吸收了不少外来的文化，在科技、宗教、文学艺术等方面都有新的发展，创造了灿烂的隋唐文化。隋唐文化是中国古代文化的高峰，也走在当时世界文化发展的前列。

大雁塔

隋唐时期各地大量兴建宫殿、寺庙、佛塔和住宅。唐朝的都城长安是当时世界上最大的城市之一。城市为长方形，外围城墙②周长36.7千米。城中五条主要街道宽百米以上。大明宫是长安最宏伟气派的建筑。隋唐时期其他著名的建

---

① 胡人——古代泛称中国北方和西方的其他民族。
② 中国古代在城的外围加筑一道外城墙。

《金刚经》局部（唐）

筑还有：河北赵县的赵州桥、陕西西安的大雁塔等。

在隋唐时期，佛教、道教得到极大传播。景教①、伊斯兰教也传入中国。唐太宗允许景教徒在长安建寺，伊斯兰教徒建立清真寺。这些外来的宗教，对中国的建筑、雕刻、绘画都有很大的影响。

在天文学方面，唐玄宗时，天文学家一行和尚测量出了子午线的长度。这是世界上最早测量子午线的记录。医学上，孙思邈（miǎo）著有《千金方》等书籍。书中收集了各种药方，总结了宝贵的医疗经验。隋唐时期，还发明了雕版印刷术，现在世界上最早的雕版印刷品《金刚经》就是唐朝印制的。

唐朝是中国诗歌的黄金时代，至今已收集了近50,000首唐代诗歌，作者达2,000多人。著名诗人有李白、杜甫和白居易等。

簪花仕女图（唐·周昉）

---

① 景教——基督教的一支。它的教义融合了波斯文化的内容，传入中国后又吸收了佛教、道教和儒家的思想。

唐朝的绘画和书法的成就也很高。著名画家吴道子有"画圣"之称；在书法艺术方面，欧阳询的"欧体"、颜真卿的"颜体"、柳公权的"柳体"风格各不相同，对后世影响很大。

生词

péng bó 蓬勃	vigorous		pàn biàn 叛变	rebell; betray
fù shù 富庶	rich		càn làn 灿烂	splendid
cì xiù 刺绣	embroidery		yǔn xǔ 允许	permit; allow
chǒng ài 宠爱	favor		zōng jiào 宗教	religion
guì fēi 贵妃	highest-ranking imperial concubine		zǐ wǔ xiàn 子午线	meridian
fèn nù 愤怒	angry; furious		xún 询	inquire
wú nài 无奈	have no way out		fēng gé 风格	style
huáng cháo 黄巢	Huang Chao (name)			

听写

蓬勃　宠爱　愤怒　无奈　叛变　灿烂　允许　宗教

风格　留学生　*富庶

注：*号以后的字词为选做题，后同。

比一比

叛 { 叛变 / 叛乱　　勃（蓬勃）/ 脖（脖子）　　奈（无奈）/ 耐（忍耐）　　允（允许）/ 充（充分）

宗 { 宗教 / 祖宗　　绣（刺绣）/ 秀（优秀）　　烂（灿烂）/ 栏（栏目）　　愤（愤怒）/ 喷（喷泉）

字词运用

愤怒
示威的人们愤怒地喊着："要和平，不要战争!"

无奈
周末准备去爬山，无奈天下雨，去不成了。

允许
请大家注意，这里不允许抽烟。

多音字

chǔ   chù
处   处
chǔ   chù
处死   到处

回答问题

1. 为什么说唐朝是中国历史上很开放的时期？那时有多少国家与唐通商？

2. 唐代，汉族和其他民族生活在一起，对文化的发展有什么好处？

3. 请说一说隋唐时期有哪些著名建筑。

4. 唐代有哪些科学技术和文化艺术成就？

词语解释

堂兄——父亲之间是兄弟，他们的儿子互称堂兄弟，年长的为堂兄。

仓皇——急忙而慌张。

处死——给予死刑处罚。

叛乱——武装叛变。

留学生——留居外国读书的学生。

云集——比喻很多人从各处来，聚集在一起。

平等——指人们在社会、政治、经济、法律等各方面受到同等对待。

阅读

飞天

敦煌莫高窟

莫高窟，俗称千佛洞，位于甘肃省河西走廊西端，敦煌市东南，在鸣沙山东麓50多米高的崖壁上，洞窟层层排列。

公元366年（前秦），一位名叫乐尊的僧人云游到此，因看到三危山金光万道，感到这里一定是佛地，便在崖壁上开凿了第一个佛窟。以后经过一代一代的修建，现在保存有北凉至元代的洞窟700多个，壁画5万多平方米，彩塑2,700多尊。

敦煌莫高窟的洞窟十之六七是隋唐时期开凿的，其中壁画内容表现了佛教故事，不少画面也反映了隋唐时期社会的繁荣。有帝王、贵族、官吏的豪华生活，有西域各族人民的形象，有中外商人贸易的情景，有农夫耕田、渔夫打鱼、船工背纤、工匠营造等劳动场面。壁画的色彩绚丽夺目，形象生动。其中，身披飘拂长带、在长空飞舞的"飞天"和"反弹琵琶"、载歌载舞的仙女，是敦煌壁画的代表作。

莫高窟的塑像，有的沉思，有的微笑，有的威严，有的勇猛，个个神情逼真，富于艺术魅力。最大的佛像高33米。著名作家余秋雨曾写到："看莫高窟，不是看死了一千年的标本，而是看活了一千年的生命。"莫高窟是一座文化艺术的宝库。

飞天

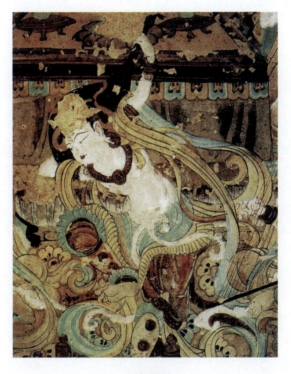

反弹琵琶

生词

dūn huáng 敦煌	Dunhuang (place)	piāo fú 飘拂	drift slightly
shān lù 山麓	foot of a mountain	fǎn tán 反弹	play (a lute) on one's back
yá bì 崖壁	cliff	pí pá 琵琶	lute
háo huá 豪华	luxurious	sù xiàng 塑像	sculpture
bēi qiàn 背纤	tow	chén sī 沉思	meditate
yíng zào 营造	construct	bī zhēn 逼真	true to life
xuàn lì duó mù 绚丽夺目	magnificent	mèi lì 魅力	charm
pī 披	wear	biāo běn 标本	specimen; sample

 English Translation

Lesson 11

Tang（Ⅱ）

After its founding, the Tang Dynasty flourished for a long time and reached its peak during more than 100 years starting from Emperor Taizong to Emperor Xuanzong of the Tang Dynasty. During this period of time, Tang was the richest and most prosperous country in the world, enjoying stable political situation, developed culture, and powerful military force.

The An-Shi Rebellion

During his late reign, Emperor Xuanzong of the Tang Dynasty lived extremely luxurious life; 700 silk weavers and embroiderers served the imperial family only. He favored Lady Yang most and didn't care about national influence. He appointed Yang Guozhong, the cousin of Lady Yang, as his Prime Minister; disorder and corruption plagued the entire country.

In 755AD, warlord An Lushan and his officer Shi Siming rebelled against Tang and soon captured the

capital city, Chang'an. This is known as the An-Shi Rebellion in history. Emperor Xuanzong fled in hurry to Sichuan; on the way of their escape, angry generals and soldiers killed Yang Guozhong and forced the emperor to put Lady Yang to death too. Emperor Xuanzong could do nothing but to have Lady Yang killed.

Then the crowned prince succeeded to the throne and became Emperor Suzong of the Tang Dynasty. The rebellion was put down after eight years of military efforts. During the period of An-Shi Rebellion, a lot of people became homeless and the field deserted; since then, the Tang Dynasty started to decline.

After the Mid-Tang Dynasty, the land-equalization system was destroyed, with officials and officers occupying a large amount of fertile fields, while more and more farmers losing lands. They became increasingly poor and were forced to rise up.

At the end of the Tang Dynasty, the Huang Chao Uprising broke out and there were more than 100,000 soldiers in the rebellious army. They swept most places in China and finally took over Chang'an. Huang Chao came to the throne and named his country Da Qi. Later on, due to the betrayal of his own general Zhu Wen, Huang Chao was defeated by Tang and retreated from the capital city before losing the final battle around Mount Tai and committing suicide.

After the failure of the Huang Chao Uprising, the local military generals enjoyed more power. In 907AD, General Zhu Wen successfully launched a coup d'état and founded the Liang Dynasty. The great empire Tang with a history of 290 years came to an end.

The Splendid Cultures in Sui and Tang Dynasties

During Sui and Tang Dynasties, both economy and culture in China were open and flourishing. The government actively communicated with foreign countries and there are more than 70 countries having trade relations with China at that time. Chang'an was not only the capital city of the Tang Dynasty but also a center in the world. Thousands of foreign businessmen and students from Korea, Japan, Persia and Eastern Roman gathered in Chang'an, Luoyang, and Guangzhou. Tang government treated them equally and allowed them to stay in China for a long time, to marry Chinese or to be officials in China. In major cities including Chang'an and Luoyang, there were many stores and restaurants operated by foreign businessmen, especially those invested by businessmen from the Western Regions. Local people could enjoy the delicious foods and the beautiful music and dancing of the Western Regions there. The colorful costumes of the Western Reginons were also favored by women of the Han nationality and Korean music was extensively popular in China. During that time, people of the Han nationality lived together with other nationalities, they communicated and exchanged with each other so that the Han nationality absorbed a lot of foreign cultures, making new progresses in technologies, religion, literature and art, creating the splendid Sui and Tang culture. Ancient Chinese culture reached its peak during Sui and Tang Dynasties and also led in the world.

A large amount of palaces, temples, pagodas and residential buildings were built during Sui and Tang Dynasties; and the capital city of the Tang Dynasty Chang'an used to be one of the biggest cities in the world at that time. The city shaped like a rectangle and the total length of its outer wall was 36.7km. There were five main streets more than 100 meters wide each and the Daming Palace was the most magnificent construction in Chang'an. Other famous architectural works during Sui and Tang Dynastyies include Zhaozhou Bridge in County Zhao, Hebei Province, and the Big Wild Goose Pagoda in Xi'an, Shaanxi Province.

Both Buddhism and Taoism flourished during Sui and Tang Dynasties, Nestorianism and Islamism were also introduced into China. Emperor Taizong of the Tang Dynasty allows Christians to build church in Chang'an and Moslems to build mosque. These foreign religions contributed a lot to Chinese architecture, sculpture, and painting.

As for astronomy, during the reign under Emperor Xuanzong of the Tang Dynasty, Master Yixing, a monk and astronomer, measured the length of meridian, which is the earliest record on the measurement of meridian in the world. In the field of medical science, Sun Simiao collected different prescriptions and summarized precious medical experience in his famous *Prescription Worth a Thousand Gold*. During Sui and Tang Dynasties, the engraving typography was invented and the earliest existing engraved work in the world, *Diamond Sutra*, was printed during the Tang Dynasty.

The Tang Dynasty is the Golden Age of poetry in China and there are nearly 50,000 poems handed down to today composed by more than 2,000 poets, including such famous names as Li Bai, Du Fu, and Bai Juyi.

The achievements of painting and calligraphy were also high in the Tang Dynasty. The prestigious painter Wu Daozi was famed as "saint painter"; in the field of calligraphy, the Ou style of Ouyang Xun, the Yan style of Yan Zhenqing, and the Liu style of Liu Gongquan have profound influence on followers till today.

Dunhuang Mogao Grottoes

Mogao Grottoes, also known as Thousand Buddha Grottoes, are located on the west end of Hexi Corridor in Gansu Province to the southeast of Dunhuang City and on 50 meter high cliff on east slope of Mingsha Mountain. These grottoes are arranged in layers.

In 366AD (during the Qianqin period) a monk named Le Zun traveled to the place and saw numerous golden rays radiating from Sanwei Mountain. Believing this must be a shrine, he cut the first grotto on the cliff. After many generations of construction, there are more than 700 grottos that can be dated back to the Kingdom of Northern Liang till the Yuan Dynasty, with murals of 50,000 square meters and more than 2,700 painted sculptures.

About 60-70 percent of Dunhuang Mogao Grottoes were constructed during Sui and Tang Dynasties; the murals depict Buddhist stories and prosperity of the time. Many murals are about the luxurious lives lived by emperors, nobleman, and officials, the images of different peoples in the Western Regions, the trading scenes of domestic and foreign businessmen, the working scenes of farmers plowing fields, fishermen catching fish, boatmen towing boats, and craftsmen producing artwork. These murals are splendidly colorful and the images are vividly depicted, among which the flying goddess with long waving ribbons dancing in the sky and the dancing fairy playing a lute on her back are masterworks representing the art of Dunhuang murals.

The sculptures of Mogao Grottoes are true to life and full of artistic charms: this one is meditating, that one is smiling; this one is august and that one looks like lionhearted. The largest Buddha statue is 33 meters high. According to Yu Qiuyu, a famous Chinese writer, "when you look at Mogao Grottoes, you're looking at lives of one thousand years old instead of specimens died some one thousand years ago." Mogao Grottoes are treasuries of culture and art.

第十二课

五代十国和北宋

唐朝灭亡后，中国又分裂成很多小国。在五十多年的时间里，五个大国先后统治了黄河一带，史称后梁、后唐、后晋、后汉、后周，合称"五代"。同一时期，在中国的南方各地先后建立了吴、南唐、楚等九个国家，加上山西一带的北汉，史称"十国"①。

公元960年，赵_{kuāng yìn}匡胤夺取后周皇帝的政权，建立宋朝，史称北宋，首都是开封。公元979年，北宋统一全国，结束了五代十国的分裂局面。

北宋建国后，宋

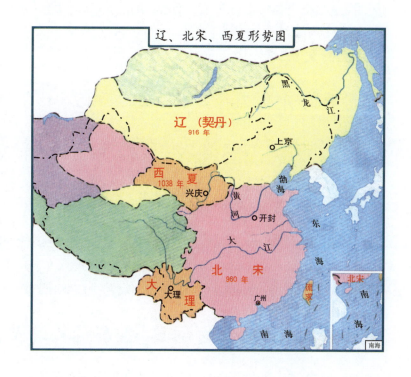

---

① 历史上把这一时期总称为"五代十国"。

太祖赵匡胤吸取了五代十国军阀分裂国家的教训,他不愿意再看见军人威胁君主,于是在一次酒宴上解除了将军们的兵权,由皇帝直接控制军队。他还建立了一套文官制度来管理国家,重文轻武的传统开始了。宋朝的科举制较为严格。经过科举,许多出身低微但有才能的人被选拔出来成为官员,而没有真才实学的人很难考上。宋朝的科举制使政府得到了很多人才,但是也渐渐形成了"万般皆下品,唯有读书高"的社会价值观念。

北宋中期,土地集中的现象很严重,全国一半农民没有土地,农民不断起义。由于对辽、夏战争的失败,宋朝不但割让了土地,每年还要向辽、夏交纳岁币,而养活军队和众多官员所需要的开支又很庞大,政府财政十分困难。面对严重的政治、社会危机,改革家王安石在皇帝的支持下于公元1069年开始变法。变法内容一是理财,二是整军。理财的办法是:国家向农民低息贷款,修水利,重新丈量土地,使税收合理。整军的办法是:减少军队数量,加强军队的战斗力。但是,王安石推行的新法受到保守派激烈的反对

听琴图(宋徽宗)

而失败。

北宋末年的皇帝宋徽宗，人称"书画皇帝"。他虽然在书画上有超人的才华，喜爱花、石、竹、木，在京城大造园林，可是治理国家，他却昏庸无能，任用奸臣，使宋末的政治十分黑暗。

与此同时，北方的女真族建立了金国。金国迅速强大起来，并于公元1125年消灭了辽国。就在灭辽的同一年，金国又出兵攻打宋。面对金兵的进攻，宋徽宗无力抵抗，将皇位让给太子（也就是后来的宋钦宗）。此时，北宋军队在抗金将领李纲的指挥下，击退了金军。但由于宋徽宗和宋钦宗的无能，一心想与金国求和，他们罢免了李纲，又答应向金国割地赔款，金军才退走。公元1127年，金军再次南下，攻占了开封，并掳走宋徽宗、宋钦宗以及皇后、妃子、大臣3,000多人和大量财物，北宋灭亡。

猛油火柜——宋朝的火焰喷射器

北宋时，虽然北方战乱不断，但是南方比较安宁，因此科学技术有明显的进步，例如：中国四大发明之一的活字印刷术出现；又由于战争的需要，火药被首次应用于军事。宋在文学艺术方面也达到了极高的水平。宋词与唐诗并称为中国古典文学艺术的瑰宝。在绘画、书法艺术上，著名画家张择端的《清明上河图》描绘了汴京（开封）清明节的情景，画面上共有将近600个人物，成为中国绘画史上一幅不朽的作品。

生词

jiě chú 解除	remove; disarm	jiān chén 奸臣	treacherous court official
jiāo nà 交纳	pay; hand in	sòng qīn zōng 宋钦宗	Emperor Qinzong of Song Dynasty
cái zhèng 财政	finance	gē dì 割地	cede territory
gǎi gé 改革	reform	lǔ zǒu 掳走	capture
dī (lì) xī 低(利)息	low interest	guī bǎo 瑰宝	gem; treasure
bǎo shǒu pài 保守派	conservative	miáo huì 描绘	describe
hūn yōng 昏庸	fatuous	bù xiǔ 不朽	immortal; enduring

听写

财政　交纳　改革　利息　描绘　割地　瑰宝　解除

不朽　税收　*奸臣

比一比

息 { 利息 / 休息 }　　财 { 财政 / 财产 }　　税 { 税收 / 纳税 }　　描 { 描绘 / 扫描 }

割 { 割断 / 割地 }　　宝 { 瑰宝 / 珠宝 }　　{ 朽（不朽）/ 巧（花言巧语）}

字词运用

结束

节日庆祝活动在人们的歌声、掌声和欢笑声中结束了。

不朽

这些英雄们建立了不朽的功勋。

回答问题

1. 请说一说王安石变法的主要内容是什么。

2. "万般皆下品,唯有读书高"的观念和科举制有没有关系?

3. "宋词与唐诗并称为中国古典文学艺术的瑰宝"这句话对吗?

词语解释

酒宴——主人请客人一起饮酒吃饭的聚会（指比较隆重的）。

税收——政府征税得到的收入。

罢免——免去官职。

赔款——战败国向战胜国赔偿(cháng)损失和作战的费用。

首次——第一次。

阅读

繁华的城镇

北宋时，虽然北方与辽国常有战争，但中原和南方人民的生活还是安定和富足的。宋朝商业发达，是当时世界上的商业大国。

宋代，由于商业和手工业的发展，在一些港口和交通要道出现了许多大大小小的城镇，形成了一个巨大的商业交换网。比如：有的城镇以生产纸和鞋为主，有的城镇印刷业很发达，有的城镇以编竹篮和竹席出名……城镇间不断进行商品交换，带动了交通的发展。那时城镇里出现了大量的流动人口，客店、酒楼、茶馆、店铺一家挨着一家，城镇里生机勃勃。

北宋的都城汴京，是当时世界上著名的大城市，有居民20万户。城内大街小巷有数不清的店铺、酒楼、饭馆，一直营业到深夜。还有"瓦肆"，是娱乐场所，那里有戏曲、杂技和武术表演。城里的夜市很热闹。天还没亮，早市又活跃起来，人来人往，非常繁华。著名的《清明上河图》，就清楚地再现了宋朝的城市生活。

清明上河图

《清明上河图》是宋朝画家张择端的作品。这幅画作在中国历史上非常著名。张择端是北宋人，他年轻的时候生活在北宋的首都汴京。他学习绘画，特别喜欢画房屋、城市、车船、河流、道路等等。

北宋灭亡后，许多人逃到南方，张择端也来到南方。回想起以前在汴京清明时节，汴河两岸的风光和人物，他十分怀念。于是他就凭着自己的记忆，把汴京各种繁华热闹的情景都一一画了出来，画成了一幅长长的画卷（全长5.25米，高0.255米）。

这画画得太好了，画的是汴京真实生活的情景。画上有汴河两岸的农田、道路和河上的桥，还有河中运粮运货的大船、小船。码头上人们不停地忙着装货、卸货。商队的骆驼、马车来来往往。路边、桥上，到处是商店，卖粮的、卖肉的、卖水果

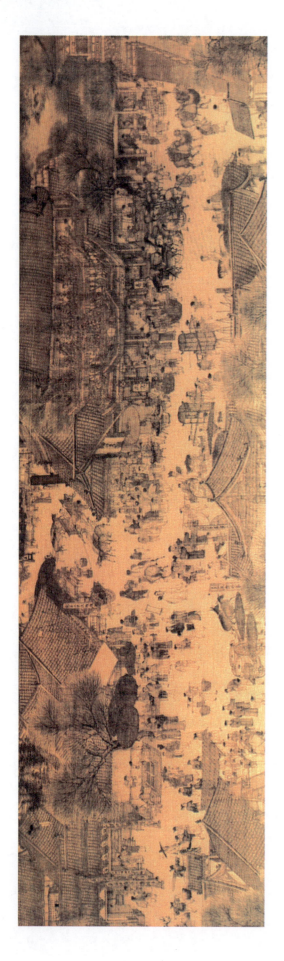
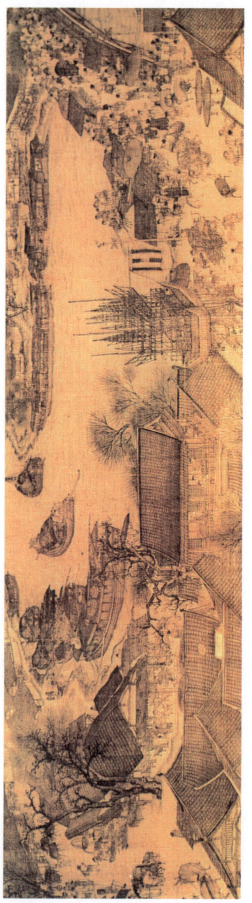

《清明上河图》局部二幅（宋·张择端）

的，还有算命的铺子……画家把汴河边商业区的热闹景象全都画出来了。

再看画面上的人物，街上有抬着花轿的迎亲队伍，有围着戏台看戏的人群，有观看和尚武术表演的大人和孩子，有在茶馆与朋友喝茶闲聊的人。再看看宫墙里面，皇后正由宫女扶着上龙船准备游湖……一切画得是那么生动、详细。

当你看这幅画的时候，就像你正在沿着汴河河岸行走，亲眼看到宋朝热闹的街市以及宫廷和平民的生活情景。这是一幅难得的历史艺术画卷。

生词

diàn pù 店铺	shop		xì qǔ 戏曲	traditional opera
shēng jī bó bó 生机勃勃	dynamic; full of vitality		zá jì 杂技	acrobatics
biàn jīng 汴京	Bianjing (the capital city of the Northern Song Dynasty)		wǔ shù 武术	martial arts
			mǎ tou 码头	dock
xiàng 巷	lane		xiè huò 卸货	discharge cargo
yíng yè 营业	do business		suàn mìng 算命	fortune-telling
sì 肆	another name for shop in the Northern Song Dynasty		xián liáo 闲聊	chat
			gōng tíng 宫廷	court
yú lè 娱乐	entertainmeat		nán dé 难得	rare

Lesson 12

Five Dynasties and Ten Kingdoms and the North Song Dynasty

After the ending of the Tang Dynasty, China split into many small states. During more than five decades after Tang, five larger states controlled the areas along the Yellow River in succession and are known as Five Dynasties of Later Liang, Later Tang, Later Jin, Later Han, and Later Zhou. During the same period, nine kingdoms founded in South China including Wu, Southern Tang and Chu, together with Northern Han in Shanxi, are known as Ten Kingdoms in history.

In 960AD, Zhao Kuangyin seized power from the emperor of Later Zhou and founded the Song Dynasty, known as the Northern Song Dynasty in history, with the capital city of Kaifeng. In 979AD, the Northern Song Dynasty unified the entire country and ended the splitting period of Five Dynasties and Ten Kingdoms.

After founding the Northern Song Dynasty, Zhao Kuangyin, the first emperor of the Song Dynasty, learned lessons from Five Dynasties and Ten Kingdoms featuring warlords splitting country and didn't want to see emperor being threatened by military generals again. He then disarmed all his generals at a banquet and ruled army directly himself. He also constructed a complete civil official system to administrate country, starting the tradition of emphasizing administrative merits instead of military achievements. The imperial examination system during the Song Dynasty was relatively strict. With this system, many low-born talented persons were selected to be officials and those without genuine ability and learning could not make it. This system helped the government to get many talents, but also contributed to the formation of a social value: no life deserves to be praised; only scholars are noble cut.

In the middle of Northern Song Dynasty, the degree of land concentration was extremely high and a half of farmers didn't have their own land, resulting in many farmer uprisings. Due to its failures in the wars against Liao and Xia, Song government had to ceded territory and offered tributes annually to both Liao and Xia. To make things worse, it required a lot of money to support both military force and numerous officials, making the government suffer financial difficulties. Facing serious political and social crisis, and with the support of the emperor, reformist Wang Anshi started reform in 1069AD. The reform mainly focused on financial and military management. As for financial reform, the state offered low-interest loan to farmers, constructed water conservancy projects, re-measured the area of land to make taxation more reasonable; as for military reform, the state reduced the amount of soldiers and improved military combat power. But, due to severe objection of the conservatives, the reform measures promoted by Wang Anshi ended in failure.

During the late Northern Song Dynasty, Emperor Huizong was known for his painting and calligraphy. He was extremely talented in art field, loved flowers, stones, bamboo, and woods, ordered to construct gardens in a large scale in the capital city; but at the same time, he was hopeless in ruling a country and

trusted the treacherous persons, resulting in a dark period politically at the end of the Northern Song Dynasty.

Meanwhile, Nuzhen nationality founded the Jin Kingdom in the north, which grew rapidly and destroyed the Kingdom of Liao in 1125AD. During the same year after defeating Liao, Jin sent army to fight with Song. Facing the attack of Jin, Emperor Huizong had no way to fight back and abdicated the throne to his crowned prince (later known as Emperor Qinzong). Under the leadership of General Li Gang, the Northern Song army defeated Jin. But incompetent Emperor Huizong and Qinzong wanted to make peace with Jin; they dismissed Li Gang and promised to cede territory and pay indemnities. So Jin retreated. But in 1127AD, Jin once again marched toward the south, took over Kaifeng and seized both Emperor Huizong and Qinzong, together with over 3,000 people including empresses, imperial concubines, ministers, officials, and a large amount of fortunes. The Northern Song Dynasty came to an end.

During the Northern Song Dynasty, although continuous wars plagued the north, south China enjoyed more peace and allowed obvious progress of science and technology. For example, one of the Four Great Inventions, the moveable-type printing technique was invented, and due to the needs of war, gunpowder was put into military use for the first time during this period. The literary and artistic achievements during this period are also great, the Song Ci poetry enjoys the same great fame with poetry produced during the Tang Dynasty and is precious Chinese classical literary treasure. As for the art of painting and calligraphy, famous painter Zhang Zeduan's *Chinese Symphonic Picture Riverside Scene at Qingming Festival* depicts scenes of Bianjing (Kaifeng) during the festival and nearly 600 figures at the time, is a great work in the history of Chinese painting.

Flourishing Cities

During the Northern Song Dynasty, although the north fought with Liao frequently, yet people in central plains and in south could still live peaceful and affluent life. The commerce during the Song Dynasty was developed and it was a business giant in the world at that time.

During the Song Dynasty, due to its developed business and handicraft industry, there formed a lot of cities of different scale in ports and around main traffic hubs, creating a large business exchanging network. For example, some cities and towns were famous for paper products and shoes, some enjoyed developed printing industry, and some others were famous for making bamboo baskets and matting ... The exchanges of commodities among these cities and towns promoted the development of traffic system. At that time, there were a large amount of floating population, with numerous hotels, restaurants, tea houses, and shops one after another, creating many flourishing and lively cities and towns.

The capital city of Bianjing during the Northern Song Dynasty was a famous big city in the world at that time, with 200,000 households and numerous shops, hotels, and restaurants open late into deep night. There were also entertainment places named "Wa Si" where people could enjoy opera, acrobat and martial art performances. The city remained lively during night and morning markets started even before the sun rose, hustling and bustling with businesses. The famous painting, *Chinese Symphonic Picture Riverside Scene at Qingming Festival*, vividly depicted city life of the Song Dynasty.

Chinese Symphonic Picture Riverside Scene at Qingming Festival

Chinese Symphonic Picture Riverside Scene at Qingming Festival by famous painter Zhang Zeduan during the Song Dynasty is very famous in the history of China. Zhang Zeduan lived during the Northern Song Dynasty and used to live in the capital city of Bianjing when he was young. He learned to paint and especially favored such themes of houses, cities, vehicles, boats, rivers and roads.

After the ending of the Northern Song Dynasty, many people fled to the south, and Zhang Zeduan was also one of them. Recalling the natural views and people along the Bianhe River during Qingming Festival in Bianjing, he missed hometown very much and painted out of his memories all these flourishing scenes in Bianjing. The scroll is 5.25m long and 0.255m high.

The picture is well painted and reproduces the true life in Bianjing. Along both banks of the Bianhe River, there are farming land, roads, bridges across the river, and boats of different sizes transporting grains and commodities in river. Workers on docks are busy loading and unloading cargos, camels and horse-drawn carriages come and go busy doing business. Shops and stores selling grains, meat, and fruits are everywhere; there is even a fortune-teller among the crowd ... The painter drew the business district along the Bianhe River bustling with different kinds of activities.

As for the people in the painting, there is a wedding team centering on a bridal sedan chair, a group of people gathering around a stage for performance, adults and kids enjoying the martial art performance of a monk, and people drinking tea and chatting with friends at a tea house. Inside the imperial palace wall, the empress is to board the dragon boat touring the lake with the help of court maids… All details are vividly depicted.

When you look at the scroll, it seems that you're actually walking along the Bianhe River and see with your own eyes a flourishing street as well as the life of ordinary people and imperial family of the Song Dynasty. It is really a precious scroll with both historic and artistic values.

第十三课

辽、西夏、金与南宋

宋朝当时的主要敌人有三个：辽国、西夏、金国。

辽是契丹人建立的。契丹族是中国古代北方的少数民族，原住在辽河一带，以游牧和渔猎为生。唐末，许多中原汉人因躲避战

乱而迁移到契丹境内。他们带去了先进的生产技术和汉族文化，使契丹人学会了种田、纺织、冶铁、建房屋，开始了农耕和定居的生活。除此之外，契丹人深受汉文化影响，创造了文字，建立孔庙并尊儒学。 公元907年，契丹八部落统一。公元916年契丹人建立国家机构并立年号，后把国名改为辽。辽国很快强大起来。公元1004年，辽军20万南下攻宋，宋真宗亲自出征，结果双方

议和，规定：宋每年给辽白银10万两，绢20万匹；边境维持现状。公元1125年，辽国被金国消灭。

《出行图》局部
（辽墓壁画）

西夏是由西北地区一个少数民族党项族建立的。五代时，党项族首领李元昊(hào)建立夏（史称西夏）。李元昊注意学习先进的汉文化和宋朝的制度，并命人创造了西夏文字。西夏、宋之间经常发生战争，后双方议和，西夏对宋称臣，宋朝每年给西夏白银7.2万两，绢15.3万匹，茶3万斤。从此西夏和宋朝之间和平了。公元1227年，西夏被蒙古消灭。

妙音鸟（西夏王陵出土）

金国是女真族建立的。女真族居住在长白山和黑龙江一带，受辽的控制。女真人不甘心受辽的压迫，起兵反辽，于公元1115年建立金国。十年后，金国军队消灭了辽国，占领了辽的土地。

在消灭辽国后，金看到了北宋的腐败无能，开始进攻宋。公元1126年年底，金军攻占宋的都城汴京，宋钦宗投降。公元1127年，金军俘虏了宋朝皇帝徽宗、钦宗父子，北宋灭亡。

宋徽宗的另一个儿子于公元1127年在临安（今杭州）继承皇位，建立南宋，他就是宋高宗。南宋朝廷害怕金兵，只想偏安求和，不想返回中原了。可是中原的人民纷纷拿起武器组成抗金义军。著名将领韩世忠、岳飞等多次打败金军。特别是岳飞领导的"岳家军"，勇猛善战，收复了大片失地。正当抗金斗争顺利发展的时候，宋高宗和宰相秦桧(huì)，害怕抗金力量壮大起来会威胁自己的统治，于是，一边下命令停止北伐，召回岳飞，一边向金求和。岳飞一回到临安就被宋高宗解除了兵权。秦桧还以谋反罪将岳飞杀害。岳飞英勇抗金的一生，得到了广大人民的尊敬。

金和南宋长期战争，双方都被削弱。这使北方的蒙古族有机会发展状大起来。蒙古骑兵与金军交战，节节胜利。公元1234年，蒙古军队消灭了金国。

成吉思汗的孙子忽必烈于公元1271年建立元朝。接着，元军向南宋

《岳飞抗金》 王金泰 画

发动进攻并占领了都城临安，统一了全中国。但是南宋的大臣文天祥等人继续抵抗。后来，文天祥被元军捉住，他视死如归，写下了千古流芳的诗句"人生自古谁无死，留取丹心照汗青"，然后从容就义。

公元1279年，宋军在广东最后战败，南宋灭亡。

两宋技术和文化的发展

宋朝长期受辽、西夏和金的侵略，军力不及强邻，但是经济文化发达，水平远在这些民族之上。

两宋时期虽然战争不断，但是生产还是有所发展，科学技术也有明显的进步。例如宋朝的陶瓷业和造船业都很先进，宋还有当时世界第一的采矿业和冶铁业。发明于唐代的火药到宋朝时已广泛应用，比欧洲使用火药早了300年。

火箭与突火枪

官窑琮式瓶

宋代，生产工具有了改进，又推广种植占城稻，增加了水稻产量。当时茶成为主要的经

交子（宋）

济作物，制茶业也相当发达，茶叶成为与少数民族交易的主要商品。另外，纺织、造纸、印刷等行业都有显著发展，特别是毕升发明了活字印刷术，大大提高了印刷速度。北宋还出现了世界上最早的纸币——交子，比欧洲发行的钞票早600多年。

生词

qì dān 契丹	Qidan (nationality)	
wéi chí 维持	maintain	
dǎng xiàng 党项	Dangxiang (nationality)	
fú lǔ 俘虏	captive; capture	
běi fá 北伐	northern expedition	
zhào huí 召回	recall	
wén tiān xiáng 文天祥	Wen Tianxiang (name)	
qiān gǔ liú fāng 千古流芳	leave a good name to posterity	
cóng róng 从容	calm	
jiù yì 就义	die a hero's death	
qīn lüè 侵略	invade; aggress	
yìng yòng 应用	apply; put to use	
tuī guǎng 推广	extend; popularize	
fā xíng 发行	issue	
chāo piào 钞票	banknote	

听写

边境　维持　党项族　钞票　从容　应用　召回

千古流芳　北伐　*俘虏　推广

比一比

境 { 边境 / 环境　　维 { 维持 / 维生素　　钞（钞票）/ 吵（争吵）　　祥（文天祥）/ 详（详细）

容 { 从容 / 容易　　略 { 侵略 / 谋略　　召（召回）/ 招（招呼）　　芳（千古流芳）/ 方（方向）

字词运用

顺利

小芳顺利地通过了考试。

应用

计算机技术得到普遍的应用。

多音字

应 yìng　　应 yīng

应用 yìng　　应该 yīng

回答问题

1. 辽、西夏和金分别是什么民族建立的国家？

2. 岳飞是南宋最著名的抗金将领，请说一说关于他的故事。

3. 文天祥被金军捉住后，他怎样面对死亡？

4. 请举例说一说两宋科技、文化发展的情况。

词语解释

边境——靠近边界的地方。

压迫——用权力或势力强制别人服从。

谋反——暗中谋划反叛。

视死如归——把死看作回家一样。形容不怕死。

阅读

民族英雄岳飞

岳飞（1103—1142），河南汤阴人，少年的时候勤奋好学，练出了一身好武艺，在抗金战斗中立下很多战功，升为元帅。人们把岳飞的军队叫做"岳家军"。"岳家军"作战勇敢，收复了郑州、洛阳等地。金军对他们十分害怕。

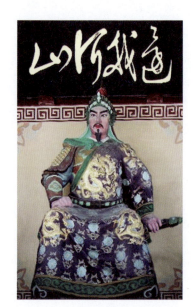

岳飞像

岳飞一生，亲自指挥打了126仗，从来没有失败过，是名副其实的常胜将军。一次，岳飞与金军铁骑兵作战，大破敌军。金军士兵感叹道："撼山易，撼岳家军难。"

正当岳飞招兵买马，积极准备渡过黄河，打败金军，收复失地的时候，宋高宗连发十二道金牌，命令岳飞退兵。岳飞无可奈何，只好挥泪班师。岳飞回到临安以后，马上就被解除了兵权。高宗和秦桧派人向金求和，金兀术要求"必先杀岳飞，方可议和"。秦桧诬陷岳飞谋反，将岳飞关进监狱毒死，那年岳飞仅仅

三十九岁。他的儿子岳云也同时被害。

岳飞一生文武双全,品德高尚,热爱祖国,千百年来被人们称做英雄;而杀害他的奸臣秦桧,则世代被人唾骂。

生词

qín fèn 勤奋	diligent	jīn wù zhū 金兀术	with draw troops from the front
zhǐ huī 指挥	command	qín huì 秦桧	Jin Wuzhu (name)
míng fù qí shí 名副其实	live up to one's reputation	wū xiàn 诬陷	Qin Hui (name)
hàn 撼	shake	tuò mà 唾骂	frame; incriminate an innocent person
jīn pái 金牌	gold plaque (issued to generals as imperial authorization for		spit on and curse
bān shī 班师	troop movement in ancient China); gold medal		

33

Lesson 13

Liao, West Xia, Jin, and the Southern Song Dynasty

The Song government had to deal mainly with three enemies at the time: the Kingdom of Liao, the West Xia, and the Kingdom of Jin.

Liao was founded by Qidan people, a minority living in the north of ancient China. They used to live around the Liaohe River, were nomads living on fishing and hunting. During the late Tang Dynasty, many people of Han nationality living in the central plains moved to the territory claimed by Qidan in order to avoid wars and thus brought along with them the advanced production technologies and culture of Han nationality. Since then, Qidan people learned farming, weaving, smelting, and building houses, settling down for farming. In addition, with profound impact of the culture of Han nationality, Qidan people invented written language, constructed temples dedicated to Confucius, and respected Confucianism. In 907AD, the eight tribes of Qidan nationality were unified. Qidan people founded their own kingdom in 916AD and then changed the name to Liao. The Kingdom of Liao grew rapidly and in 1004AD, it sent 200,000 army to the south attacking Song, forcing Emperor Zhenzong of the Song Dynasty onto the battlefield himself. Later on, they made peace with each other on the condition that Song government offered to Liao each year 100,000 *liang* of silver and 200,000 *pi* of thin silk. The border resumed peace; in 1125AD, Liao was destroyed by the Kingdom of Jin.

West Xia was founded by Dangxiang nationality, a minority in northwestern area. During the period of Five Dynasties, Li Yuanhao, the chief of Dangxiang nationality at the time, founded Xia (known as West Xia in history). Li Yuanhao learned advanced culture of Han nationality and systems of the Song Dynasty, and ordered to invent the written language of West Xia. West Xia fought with Song frequently and finally made peace with each other. West Xia submitted to the Song on the condition that Song government offered each year to West Xia 72,000 *liang* of silver, 153,000 *pi* of thin silk, and 30,000 *jin* of tea. Peace maintained between West Xia and Song until West Xia was destroyed by Mongolia in 1227AD.

The Kingdom of Jin was founded by Nuzhen nationality living in the area of Changbai Mountain and Heilongjiang River. It was once controlled by Liao and, being reluctant to be oppressed by Liao, fought with Liao and founded the Kingdom of Jin in 1115AD. Ten years later, the army of Jin destroyed Liao and took over all its territory.

After destroying Liao and witnessing the corruption and incompetence of the Northern Song government, Jin started to attack Song. At the end of 1126AD, Jin seized the capital city Bianjing and Emperor Qinzong of the Song Dynasty surrendered. In 1127AD, Jin captured Emperor Huizong and Qinzong; and the Northern Song Dynasty came to an end.

Another son of Emperor Huizong came to the throne in 1127AD in Lin'an (today's Hangzhou) and founded the Southern Song Dynasty; this is Emperor Gaozong of the Song Dynasty. The Southern Song

government was afraid of Jin and eager to make peace instead of fighting back to the central plains. But people in the central plains rose to take arms and organize army against Jin. Well-known generals Han Shizhong and Yue Fei defeated the army of Jin many times. The Army of Yue Family led by Yue Fei was especially good at fighting and recovered a lot of lost territory. Just as the fight against Jin went through smoothly and fruitfully, since Emperor Gaozong and Prime Minister Qin Hui were afraid that the increasingly powerful force against Jin would threaten their rule, they ordered to stop the expedition to the north and call Yue Fei back to the court. Meanwhile, they engaged in the negotiation with Jin. At his coming back to Lin'an, Yue Fei was disarmed by Emperor Gao Zong and killed by Qin Hui under the false charge of conspiring against imperial rule. Dedicating his life to fighting against Jin, Yue Fei gained respects among ordinary people.

After engaging in wars for a long period of time, both Jin and Southern Song declined, giving Mongolia nationality in the north an opportunity to grow rapidly. Mongolian cavalry fought with and defeated Jin; in 1234AD, the Mongolia destroyed the Kingdom of Jin.

Kublai Khan, the grandson of Genghis Khan, founded the Yuan Dynasty in 1271AD and then attacked Southern Song, captured the capital city of Lin'an and unified the entire country. But Minister Wen Tianxiang and other people of Southern Song continuously fought back until Wen Tianxiang was captured by Yuan. He faced death unflinchingly and left a well-known poem: "Everyone will die at last; but I'll leave a loyal heart shining in the pages of history." He died in the way he advocated in the poem.

In 1279AD, the army of Song lost the final battle in Guangdong and the Southern Song Dynasty came to the end.

Technological and Cultural Development during two Song Dynasties

Song was invaded by Liao, West Xia, and Jin for a long period of time and suffered inferior military power; but its economy and culture were developed and superior than these minorities.

During the two Song Dynasties, the country suffered continuous wars but still managed to develop in production, with obvious progressing of science and technology. For example, both ceramic industry and ship-building industry during the Song Dynasty were highly developed; its mining industry and smelting industry ranked the first in the world at that time. Gunpowder invented during the Tang Dynasty was extensively applied during sht Song Dynasty, which was 300 earlier than Europe.

During the Song Dynasty, production tools were greatly improved; the output of rice increased greatly due to the extensive promotion of Zhancheng rice. Tea became one of the leading economic crops at the time and tea industry was extremely developed, making tea leaves the main commodity traded with minorities. In addition, textile, paper-making and printing industries also progressed considerably, especially after the invention of moveable-type printing technique by Bi Sheng, the printing speed rose greatly. The Northern Song Dynasty also produced the first paper money, *jiao-zi*, in the world, which was 600 years earlier than the bill issued in Europe.

Yue Fei, a National Hero

Yue Fei (1103-1142) was born in Tangyin, Henan. He was diligent and eager to learn when he was young, was especially good at martial art. He was promoted to be supreme commander due to numerous merits in battles against Jin and people called his men "Army of Yue Family". He led his valiant army recover Zhengzhou and Luoyang; Jin was extremely afraid of them.

During his lifetime, Yue Fei commanded a total of 126 battles and was never defeated by enemies, winning him the fame of "Ever-Victorious General". One day, Yue Fei led his men fighting with and defeated the cavalry of Jin. His enemy sighed: "To move a mountain much easier than defeating the Army of Yue Family."

When Yue Fei was recruiting men and buying horses, preparing actively for crossing the Yellow River, defeating Jin, and recovering lost territory, he was ordered to return twelve times in the form of twelve gold plaques by Emperor Gaozong. Yue Fei could do nothing but retreating. Coming back to Lin'an, Yue Fei was immediately disarmed. Meanwhile, Emperor Gaozong and Qin Hui sent messenger to make peace with Jin, while Jin Wuzhu insisted on "killing Yue Fei before making any negotiation." Qin Hui then maliciously prosecuted Yue Fei for conspiring against imperial rule and threw him in prison before poisoning him. Yue Fei was only 39 when he died and his son Yue Yun was also killed.

Yue Fei was good at both letters and martial arts; being noble and loving his home country, he has been respected as a hero for more than one thousand years, while Qin Hui, the treacherous court official persecuted him, was spit and cursed for generations.

第十四课

成吉思汗和他的子孙

成吉思汗像

蒙古族本来是一个生活在蒙古草原上的游牧民族。12世纪时，蒙古的各个部落之间战争不断，其中一个部落打败了其他部落，成为最强大的部落，这个部落的首领叫铁木真。公元1206年，蒙古部落首领大会推举铁木真为成吉思汗①，从此蒙古建立了统一的政权，创造了蒙古文字。

蒙古的强大是有原因的。蒙古人生活在土地贫瘠，气候严寒的漠北②。他们依靠骑射的本领奔驰在草原上，练成了吃苦、尚武的精神。同时，蒙古成长壮大的时候，四周没有强国。邻近的宋、金、西夏之间常年打仗，互相削弱；西亚各国处在长期混乱之中；东罗马帝国衰落以后，欧洲没有统一的国家。这一切给了成吉思汗一个绝好的机会。公元1219年，成吉思汗率领蒙古军队

---

① 成吉思汗——成吉思，蒙语，意思是"强大"；"汗"是可汗的简称。
② 漠北——古代指蒙古高原大沙漠以北地区。

进行了第一次西征，占领了今俄罗斯至伊朗西北境的广大地区。他又带领蒙古骑兵于公元1227年消灭了西夏。在蒙古军队就要攻克西夏的时候，65岁的成吉思汗病死。

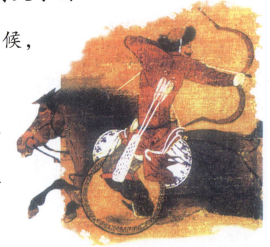

蒙古骑兵

成吉思汗死后，他的第三个儿子窝阔台继承了汗位。公元1234年蒙古又灭了金国。公元1235年至1244年，蒙古军队又进行了一次西征。成吉思汗的一个孙子拔都，率兵征服了今俄罗斯、匈牙利等地，一直打到柏林附近和亚得里亚海滨，震动了整个欧洲。成吉思汗的另一个孙子旭烈兀于公元1253年至1259年第三次西征。他攻占了巴格达等地，建立了伊儿汗国①。成吉思汗的子孙们又继续南征，打败了南宋等许多国家，建立了地跨欧亚的蒙古大帝国，国土面积有3,000多万平方公里。蒙古帝国东起白令海峡，西到莱

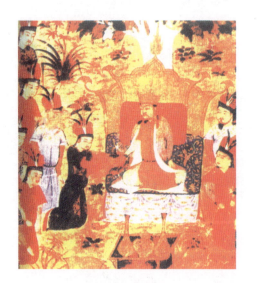

窝阔台即位图

---

① 伊儿汗国——有的史书也称为"伊利汗国"。

茵河，北到北冰洋，南到波斯湾。其领土除了今天的中国和蒙古外，还包括了朝鲜半岛、俄罗斯、东欧、伊朗、伊拉克、土耳其、缅甸、巴基斯坦等国家。但是，到成吉思汗的孙子辈时，蒙古帝国实际上已分为元帝国和四大汗国。

公元1260年，成吉思汗的孙子忽必烈继位，史称元世祖。公元1271年，改国号为"大元"并迁都(dū)大都（今北京），从此，北京渐渐成为中国政治、经济和文化的中心。

生词

游牧 yóu mù	nomadic	北冰洋 běi bīng yáng	the Arctic Ocean
奔驰 bēn chí	run quickly	伊朗 yī lǎng	Iran
混乱 hùn luàn	chaos	伊拉克 yī lā kè	Iraq
匈牙利 xiōng yá lì	Hungary	土耳其 tǔ ěr qí	Turkey
旭烈兀 xù liè wù	Hulagu (name)	缅甸 miǎn diàn	Myanmar
跨 kuà	extend across	巴基斯坦 bā jī sī tǎn	Pakistan
莱茵河 lái yīn hé	Rhine River		

听写

奔驰　匈牙利　跨　北冰洋　伊朗　伊拉克　缅甸　混乱

巴基斯坦　征服　*旭烈兀　莱茵河

比一比

征 { 征服 / 征兵 / 出征 　　游 { 游牧 / 旅游 / 游泳 　　联 { 联盟 / 联合 / 联系 　　洋 { 北冰洋 / 太平洋 / 得意洋洋

基 { 巴基斯坦 / 基础 　　伊 { 伊拉克 / 伊朗 　　跨（跨越）/ 夸（夸奖）　　匈（匈牙利）/ 胸（胸有成竹）

字词运用

本领

他射击的本领高强，百发百中。

跨

刘翔飞快地跨越一个个栏架，冲向终点，取得冠军。（xiáng）

世界上很多大公司都是跨国公司。

回答问题

1. 元朝的首都是现在的哪个城市?

2. 为什么蒙古能强大起来?请说一说其中的原因。

词语解释

本领——技能;能力。

吃苦——经受艰苦。

尚武——注重军事或武术。

绝好——极好;最好。

阅读

中西交通

中国对外交通,开始于汉代的丝绸之路。到了隋唐,对外交通除了陆路还有海路。宋代陆路交通中断,但海路贸易繁荣。元代蒙古人征服了很多的民族,国土空前辽阔,各民族之间语言不通,但是在当时,如果一个人通晓蒙古语,可由欧洲到达中国,一路之上交流毫无阻碍。自此,"世界"大通,东西文化互相影响。中国的发明西传,西方近代文化开始东来。

元政府在交通大道上修建驿站。每隔几十里设一个驿站,给宣布政令的人员和来往的商人们提供食宿和喂马的草料。东西大道长一万多里,沿途都有驿站,所以政令的发布和商旅的往来都很方便、畅通。据说,还有一条通过云南去阿拉伯半岛的陆路。至于海道,自元世祖允许国际商贸往来以后,商船从中国沿海出发经印度洋可以到达波斯湾。中国在广州、杭州、温州、泉州设立了七个市舶司,管理中外贸易。大都成为国际性都市,泉州成为当时世界上最大的海港。海运业一时特别发达。

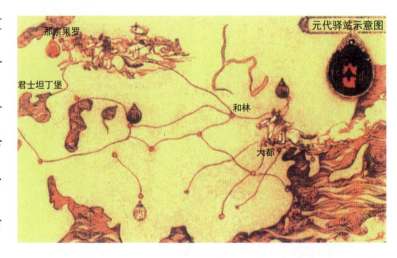

生词

tōng xiǎo 通晓	thoroughly understand	chàng tōng 畅通	unblocked
zǔ ài 阻碍	hinder; obstacle	bàn dǎo 半岛	peninsula
xuān bù 宣布	declare; announce	shì bó sī 市舶司	Maritime Trade Supervisory Department
tí gōng 提供	provide	yì shí 一时	a period of time

Lesson 14

Genghis Khan and His Descendants

Mongolia nationality used to be a nomad living on Mongolian grassland. In the 12th century, wars broke out among different Mongolian tribes. Finally, one tribe defeated others and became the most powerful, the chieftain of the tribe named Temujin. In 1206AD, on the conference held by Mongolian chieftains, Temujin was elected as Genghis Khan; since then, Mongolia became a unified entity with newly invented written language.

There were reasons behind the rising of Mongolia. Mongolians lived in the north desert area where the land was barren and climate was frigid. They lived on the grassland depending on their riding skill and archery, fostering the tough character and spirit of warriors. Moreover, during the process of its growing, there was no powerful force around. Its neighbors of Song, Jin, and West Xia fought with each other continuously and therefore became declining. Countries in West Asia also suffered disorder for a long period of time. After the declining of Eastern Roman, there was no unified country in Europe. All these provided a good opportunity for Genghis Khan. In 1219AD, Genghis Khan led his Mongolian army for the first expedition to the west and took over a vast area of today's Russia to the northwest border of Iran. He then led Mongolian cavalry destroy West Xia in 1227AD; just when his army was about to seize West Xia, Genghis Khan died of illness at the age of 65.

After the death of Genghis Khan, his third son Ogodei Khan succeeded to the throne. In 1234AD, Mongolia destroyed the Kingdom of Jin; during 1235AD to 1244AD, Mongolian army launched another expedition to the west. Batu Khan, a grandson of Genghis Khan, led army and conquered today's Russia and Hungary, marching till the place close to Berlin and the Adriatic Coast, shaking the entire Europe. Hulagu Khan, another grandson of Genghis Khan, led the third expedition to the west during 1253AD to 1259AD. He took over Baghdad and founded the Kingdom of Il-Khan. The descendants of Genghis Khan continuously explored to the south and defeated many countries there including Southern Song, founding the great Mongolian Empire spanning both Europe and Asia with a total territory of more than 30 million square kilometers. The Empire of Mongolia covered an extensive area bordering the Bering Strait in the east, the Rhine River in the west, the Arctic Ocean in the north , and the Persian Gulf in the south. Apart from today's China and Mongolia, its territory also included Korean Peninsular, the Russia, East Europe, Iran, Iraq, Turkey, Burma, and Pakistan. In the hands of the grandsons of Genghis Khan, however, the Empire of Mongolia was actually divided into the Empire of Yuan and four Kingdoms of Khan.

In 1260AD, Kublai Khan, the grandson of Genghis Khan, succeeded the throne and was later known as Emperor Shizu of the Yuan Dynasty. In 1271AD, the Dynasty was renamed "Da Yuan" and moved its capital city to Dadu (today's Beijing). Since then, Beijing has become political, economic, and cultural center of China.

Communications between China and the West

The out-going communications in China started from the Silk Road during the Han Dynasty. During Sui and Tang Dynasties, apart from land route, seaborne communication route was also developed. During the Song Dynasty, the land route stopped but marine trade became flourishing. During the Yuan Dynasty the Mongolian conquered literally numerous nationalities and enjoyed unprecedented vast territory. Different nationalities spoke their own languages, but at that time, a person proficient at Mongolian could reach China from Europe without any obstacle in communication. Since then, the world became close with western and eastern cultures actively interacting with each other. Chinese inventions were passed to the west and the modern western cultures also influenced the east world.

The Yuan government built post houses along main roads. There was one post house every dozens of *li*, providing accommodation for staff delivering government orders and businessmen as well as feeding their horses. The main east-west road at the time was 10,000 *li* long with post houses along the road, making it convenient and smooth for the distribution of government orders and for traveling businessman. It is said that there was another land rout ereaching Arabia through Yunnan. As for marine route, since Emperor Shizu of the Yuan Dynasty allowed international business exchanges, merchant ship could start from the coastal area of China and reach Persian Gulf by crossing the Indian Ocean. China established seven Maritime Trade Supervisory Departments in Guangzhou, Hangzhou, Wenzhou, and Quanzhou to regulate foreign trade. Dadu became an international metropolitan and Quanzhou was the biggest seaport in the world. Maritime industry flourished greatly at that time.

第十五课

元

忽必烈像

忽必烈建立的元朝是蒙古族的王朝，也是中国历史上第一个少数民族统治全国的政权。在中国历史上，元朝的疆土比以往任何朝代都要辽阔。忽必烈是一位杰出的皇帝，他清楚地看到，在成吉思汗赫赫武功的背后，是蒙古人治理国家经验的不足和观念的落后。于是他重用汉人，大力推行汉法，使元朝面貌一新。

为了管理这个辽阔的国家，元朝建立了行省制度：中央设中书省管理全国政务；地方设行省，皇帝派官员管理。行省制

度使边远地区和内地一样，受到国家的管理并向国家交纳赋税。

元朝时，今天的西藏成为元的正式行政区。那里有元朝官员清查户口和收税。公元1360年，元朝设立了澎湖巡检司，管理澎湖列岛和琉(liú)球（今台湾）。

忽必烈还实行劝农的政策，使农业得到恢复和发展。蒙古族本是一个游牧民族，进入黄河流域农业区以后，他们把汉人赶走，让田地长出绿草，好放牧牛羊。但是忽必烈却下令保护农业，把牧场退还为农田；还成立了"劝农司"，专门劝老百姓开垦田地，种桑养蚕，从而使农业生产不断恢复和发展。

忽必烈提倡以儒学为主的汉族传统文化。他年轻时就受到儒家文化的影响，常请儒士来讲解儒学的道理。继位以后，他下令建立孔庙，恢复学校，还设立国子学，用汉族文化教育蒙古官员的子弟。正是由于忽必烈大力推行汉法，才使草原上建立起来的大蒙古国终于转变成了元王朝。

马可·波罗告别元世祖回国

中统元宝交钞——元代纸币

元朝中期，海外贸易空前发达。由于东西方来往的道路通行无阻，欧亚之间的商业活动相当活跃。中国的印刷术、火药等传到西方，西方文化也随着商人传到中国。那时的北京，有许多外国商人和使节长期居住。元代，意大利人马可·波罗写了一本《马可·波罗游记》，轰动了欧洲。在这本书中，他介绍了在中国17年的经历和见闻，使欧洲人开始认识中国。此外，海运、漕运和商业的繁荣，以及纸币的流行，使元朝成为当时世界上最富庶的国家之一。

铜火铳(chòng)

元代的科学技术和文学艺术也都有发展。天文学家郭守敬制订的《授时历》推算出一年有365.2425日，与现行的公历相同。元朝，在中国南方，棉花种植已经非常普遍，出现了一大批棉纺织手工业者，其中最著名的是黄道婆。黄道婆推广、改进了纺车、织机和棉纺织技术，棉布在中国得以大量生产。元代文化最著名的是元曲，它是中国现代戏曲的开端，代表作品有关汉卿的《窦(qīng)娥(é)冤》、王实甫(fǔ)的《西厢记》等。

不过，元朝为了保住蒙古贵族的地位，实行了民族歧视和压迫的政策。元朝把全国人民分为四个等级，最高等的是蒙古人，其次为色目人，第三等为汉人，最低等的是南人①。汉人和南人在政治上、法律上或科举考试方面都受到歧视。这个政策很不得人心，也加深了民族矛盾。忽必烈死后，其后代争夺帝位的斗争激烈，加上连年灾荒，终于爆发了红巾军起义。义军领袖朱元璋（zhāng）于公元1368年在今南京称帝，建立明朝。同年，起义军攻入元大都，元朝灭亡。

明代刻本《西厢记》插图

---

① 元朝的"色目人"指中亚、西亚、欧洲以及当时吐蕃（bō）等许多民族，"汉人"主要指原金朝统治下的汉族、契丹、女真等民族，"南人"主要指原南宋统治下的人民。

生词

hè hè wǔ gōng 赫赫武功	impressive military achievements	jīng lì 经历	experience
miàn mào 面貌	appearance	cáo yùn 漕运	water transport of grain to the capital (*in feudal times*)
jiǎn chá 检(查)	examine; check	zhì dìng 制订	formulate
péng hú liè dǎo 澎湖列岛	Penghu Islands	xì qǔ 戏曲	traditional opera
kāi kěn 开垦	reclaim wasteland	dòu 窦	Dou (*surname*)
sāng 桑	mulberry	xiāng 厢	wing-room; compartment
tí chàng 提倡	advocate	qí shì 歧视	discrimination
huó yuè 活跃	vibrant	lǐng xiù 领袖	leader

听写

活跃　提倡　经历　检(查)　等级　(车)厢　以往

见闻　激烈　领袖　*开垦　澎湖

比一比

$\begin{cases} 倡（提倡） \\ 昌（许昌） \end{cases}$ $\begin{cases} 垦（开垦） \\ 肯（不肯） \end{cases}$ $\begin{cases} 检（检查） \\ 捡（捡起） \end{cases}$ $\begin{cases} 歧（歧视） \\ 枝（树枝） \end{cases}$

$\begin{cases} 订（制订） \\ 定（决定） \end{cases}$ $\begin{cases} 厢（车厢） \\ 相（相信） \end{cases}$ $\begin{cases} 跃（活跃） \\ 妖（妖精） \end{cases}$ $\begin{cases} 烈（激烈） \\ 列（排列） \end{cases}$

字词运用

见闻
你这次旅行有什么有趣的见闻？快给我们说一说吧。

激烈
大家对这个问题有各种不同的意见，争论得十分激烈。

近义词

开端——开头——开始　　　　以往——以前——过去

回答问题

1. 忽必烈为什么重用汉人？

2. 忽必烈怎样推行汉法？

3. 元代海外贸易和东西方文化交流的情况是怎样的？请具体说一说。

4. 元代文化中哪一类艺术最有成就？请举出两个例子。

词语解释

户口——住户和人口；本地区居民的身份。

空前——以前所没有。

见闻——见到和听到的。

元曲——元朝的一种戏曲形式。

激烈——（动作、言论等）剧烈。

其次——第二；顺序较后。

阅读

马可·波罗

马可·波罗像

马可·波罗是意大利人，出生在威尼斯一个商人家庭。他是一个了不起的旅行家，是第一个把地大物博的中国介绍给欧洲的人。在他的《马可·波罗游记》中，记载了中国40多个城市，还把当时中国的自然和社会情况作了详细的描述，例如：养蚕、丝绸、造纸、纸币、印刷、宫殿、都城、政府以及蒙古大汗忽必烈的节庆、游猎活动等等。

1260年，马可·波罗的父亲和叔父经商到过中国，见过大汗忽必烈。1271年，他的父亲和叔父再次动身去中国，带着马可·波罗同行。这次他们三人穿越西亚各国和中亚大沙漠，翻越世界屋脊帕米尔高原进入新疆，又在无边无际的沙漠中前行。他们一路历经千辛万苦，有时候一连十几天遇不到一户人家，空中见不到一只飞鸟，路上看不到一棵青草。就这样，他们用了三年半的时间终于到达了上都（今内蒙古多伦县），见到了元世祖忽必烈。

忽必烈见到他们非常高兴，设宴欢迎他们，并留他们居住下来。马可·波罗聪明好学，很快学会了蒙古语和汉语。忽必烈很信任他，除了让他在大都工作外，还派他到国内各地和一些邻近国家进行访问。他到过中国的大部分地区，从运河乘船去过江南。据说他还在扬州当过官。

转眼，马可·波罗和父亲、叔父在中国已经生活了17年。他们想回家乡威尼斯看看。正巧元世祖的一位公主要远嫁到伊儿汗国，他让马可·波罗父子三人护送公主从海上去，但要求他们送到以后再返回中国。马可·波罗父子带着忽必烈写给法国、英国和西班牙等国国王的书信，带领十四艘船出发了，他们用了两年半的时间才到达了伊儿汗国。之后，他们想回家看看，但是在回乡的路上听到元世祖去世的消息，后来就没有再回到中国。

公元1295年，马可·波罗回到了家乡威尼斯。当时威尼斯正在打仗，马可·波罗加入了威尼斯军队，在作战中被俘。在监狱里，他和一位作家关在一起。他把中国的故事讲给作家听，经过作家记录、整理，写出了著名的《马可·波罗游记》。

《马可·波罗游记》七百多年来在世界各地流传，译本超过了一百种。马可·波罗的著作对于人们了解亚洲的历史、地理，以及中西交通的历史，起了很大的作用。

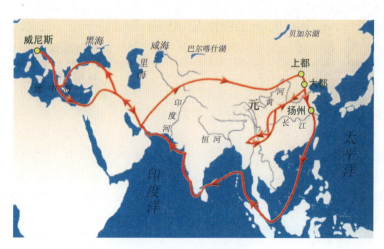

马可·波罗旅行路线图

生词

liǎo bu qǐ 了不起	great; extraordinary		xìn rèn 信任	just in time
shū fù 叔父	uncle		zhèng qiǎo 正巧	princess
wū jǐ 屋脊	ridge of a roof		gōng zhǔ 公主	arrange
pà mǐ ěr gāoyuán 帕米尔高原	Pamir Mountain Area		zhěng lǐ 整理	
	trust			

English Translation

Lesson 15

The Empire of Yuan

Kublai Khan founded the Yuan Dynasty of Mongolia nationality, the first state power ruling the entire country by minority in the history of China. In Chinese history, the territory of Yuan ranks the first among all dynasties and Kublai Khan was an outstanding emperor, who clearly realized that what lied behind the impressive military achievements of Genghis Khan was the lack of experience in administration and the lagging of concepts held by Mongolians. Therefore, he appointed officials of Han nationality to take important posts and promoted extensively the laws of Han nationality, achieving great progresses during the Yuan Dynasty.

In order to manage the country with vast territory, the Yuan government established the system of administrative provinces, regulating that the central secretariat was in charge of national affairs, while local executive secretariats (known as executive provinces or provinces) led by officials directly appointed by the emperor were in charge of local affairs. With this system, the remote regions were well administrated by the state as inland area did and paid required duties and taxes to the central government.

During the Yuan Dynasty, today's Tibet was the official executive area of the Yuan Government, where officials checked and registered permanent residence and collected taxes. In 1360AD, Penghu Inspection Office was established to administrate Penghu Islands and Liuqiu (today's Taiwan).

Kublai Khan also adopted policies in favor of farmers to recover and develop agriculture. Mongolia used to be a nomad; after entering agricultural area along the Yellow River, Mongolians drove locals of Han nationality away so that grass grew in the field and they could pasture livestock. But Kublai Khan ordered to protect agriculture and to turn farm into farming land again. He established Agriculture Development Office to persuade farmers cultivating fields, planting mulberry trees and rearing silkworms, continuously developing and promoting agricultural production.

Kublai Khan advocated traditional culture of Han nationality centering on Confucianism; he was profoundly influenced by Confucianism when he was young and often invited Confucian scholars to lecture on Confucian theories. After being the emperor, he ordered to construct Confucian temples, to restore academies, and to establish Imperial Academy and educated children of Mongolian officials and officers with the culture of Han nationality. Thanks to the promotion of laws of Han nationality by Kublai Khan, the great Kingdom of Mongolia originated from vast grassland finally evolved into the Yuan Dynasty.

In the Mid-Yuan Dynasty, overseas trade became flourishing more than ever. Due to the smooth communication between the west and the east, the business activities between Europe and Asia were vibrant. The businessmen passed printing technique and gunpowder from China to the west and introduced at the same time western culture to China. Many foreign businessmen and envoys pursued long-term stay in Beijing. At that time, Italian traveler Marco Polo wrote a book entitled *The Travels of Marco Polo* and caused a stir in Europe. In the book, he introduced his 17-year experience in China and Europeans started to know about China since then. Moreover, the flourishing seaborne trade, inland water transport and business as well as the circulating of paper money made the Yuan Dynasty one of the most populous and richest countries in the world.

During the Yuan Dynasty, both technology and art achieved great progresses. According to the Shoushi Calendar invented by astronomer Guo Shoujing, there were 365.2425 days in a year, matching exactly with current Gregorian calendar. At that time, cotton was extensively planted in Southern China and there were a lot of cotton textile handicraftsmen, among which Huang Daopo was most famous one. She improved and promoted spinning wheel, weaving machine and cotton textile technique, resulting in a large amount of cotton cloth output in China. Yuan Qu, a verse form popular in the Yuan Dynasty, served as the origin of Chinese modern opera, and its masterpieces included *Injustice to Dou E* by Guan Hanqing and *Romance of the West Chamber* by Wang Shifu.

In order to maintain the status of Mongolian nobles, however, the Yuan government adopted policies of national discrimination and oppression. The Yuan government divided the national population into four grades, leading with Mongolian and being followed by Semu people, people of Han nationality, with Southern people ranking the lowest. The last two grades of Han and Southern people were discriminated against in politics, laws, and imperial examinations. The policies were unpopular at the time and intensified national conflicts. After Kublai Khan died, his descendents fought bitterly for the throne; this, together with the impact of famine due to crop failures for years, initiated the Red-Turban Rebelling, whose leader Zhu Yuanzhang came to the throne in 1368AD in today's Nanjing and founded the Ming Dynasty. At the same year, the insurrectionists seized the capital city of Dadu and the Yuan Dynasty came to the end.

Marco Polo

Marco Polo was an Italian and born into a businessman family in Venice. He was a great traveler and the first person introducing to Europe China with vast territory and rich resources. In *The Travels of Marco Polo*, he recorded his travel in more than 40 Chinese cities, describing in details both natural and social information of China at that time, for example: silkworms rearing, silk products, paper making, printing, palaces, capital city, government, as well as festivals and hunting activities of Kublai Khan.

In 1260AD, the father and uncle of Marco Polo traveled to China on business and met with Kublai Khan. In 1271AD, his father and uncle paid another visit to China, bringing along Marco Polo together with them. This time, the three of them came across the West Asia and the desert in Middle Asia, entered Xinjiang through Pamir Mountain Area, the world ridge, before conquering the vast desert. They overcame a lot of difficulties on the way and could hardly hold a household in sight, see a flying bird in sky or a green grass on their way for a dozen of days. It took them three and a half years to reach Shangdu (today's Duolun County in Inner Mongolia) and meet Kublai Khan, Emperor Shizu of the Yuan Dynasty.

Kublai Khan was happy to meet them, treating them with banquets and asking them to stay. Marco Polo was smart and diligent and soon learned both languages of Mongolian and Chinese. Kublai Khan trusted him and, apart from offering him jobs inside Dadu, sent him to visit other domestic places and surrounding countries. Therefore, he traveled to most places in China and visited the southern area of the lower reaches of the Yangtze River on boat through the grand canal. It is said that he once served as local official in Yangzhou.

Time passed quickly and Marco Polo, together with his father and uncle, had lived in China for 17 years. They wanted to go back to their hometown Venice. It happened that Emperor Shizu of the Yuan Dynasty planned to marry one of his princesses to the Kingdom of Il-Khan; so he ordered that Marco Polo, his father and uncle to escort the princess on her seaborne journey on the condition that they should come back to China once the mission was accomplished. The three of them started the journey with 14 boats and the letters written by Kublai Khan for the kings of France, Great Britain, and Spain. It took them two and a half years to arrive at the destination. Then they wanted to go back home; and on their way home, they got the news that Emperor Shizu of the Yuan Dynasty passed away. They never came back to China later.

In 1295AD, Marco Polo came back to his hometown Venice, which was in the war at that time, and joined army. After being caught in a battle and put into prison, Marco Polo met a cellmate also a writer. He told the writer stories about China; the writer recorded what he said and composed the well-known *The Travels of Marco Polo*.

The Travels of Marco Polo became popular in the world for more than 700 years and was translated into over 100 different languages, contributing a lot for people to understand the history and geography of Asia, as well as the history of Communcation between China and the West.

第十六课

明（上）

明朝的第一个皇帝朱元璋(zhāng)，出身贫苦，做过和尚，后来参加元末红巾军起义，成为义军领袖，并于公元1368年在今南京建立明朝。他就是明太祖。

明朝建国后，朱元璋把儿子们分封到各地去做藩(fān)王，他们都带领着很多军队，其中燕(yān)王朱棣(dì)的军力最强。朱元璋死后把皇位传给了孙子建文帝。因为建文帝年纪很小，燕王朱棣起兵造反，公元1402年，他赶走建文帝，自己做了皇帝，并把首都从南京迁到了北京。

郑和宝船图

朱棣是一位胸怀大志的帝王，在他的统治下，明朝越来越强大。他曾派太监郑和带领船队出使西洋①。郑和的远航不仅使明朝的威望提高，促进了中外文化交流，而且激起了中国人向海外

---

① 西洋——当时把中国南海以西的海洋称为西洋。

发展的兴趣。从此广东、福建移民南洋的人渐渐多了起来。

北京成为明朝的首都以后，几百年来一直是中国政治、经济和文化的中心。北京的城市建筑

北京故宫

布局严整，城墙高大雄伟，街道宽阔笔直，是古代城市建筑的杰作。城市中心为皇宫，金碧辉煌，是现今世界上最大、保留最完整的古代宫殿建筑群。明朝又修复了长城。长城东起山海关①，西到嘉峪关②，全长6,000多千米，修复工程浩大。

青花束莲盘（明）

明初的政策是减轻人民的税赋，恢复和发展生产。很快，明朝农业的产量就远远超过了前代。农村多余的劳动力流入了手工业与商业，使手工业和商业发展起来。当时的手工业技术十分精巧，生产规模也不断扩大，出现了雇佣关系。例如，明朝的青花瓷十分精美，闻名于世。

---

① 山海关——地名，在今河北省秦皇岛市。
② 嘉峪关——地名，在今甘肃省嘉峪关市。

生产瓷器的景德镇，几十里内，处处有窑，雇工成百上千。经过景德镇的道路、河流沿途尽是运送瓷器的车船。当时的丝绸更是花色繁多。明朝中叶以后，江南苏杭地区丝织业特别发达，城镇居民无论男女老幼，大多进入丝织业。富人为雇主，雇有长工和短工，大的作坊

明人演戏图

有几十台织机。精美的瓷器和丝绸是中国主要的出口商品，销售到欧洲和美洲，换取了大量的白银。那时候，明朝在国际贸易中获得的是顺差。

明朝的时候，中国的传统科学技术仍然处于世界领先的地位。当时的科学家写出了三部科学巨著：《本草纲目》、《农政全书》和《天工开物》。《本草纲目》是著名药物学家、医学家李时珍用27年时间完成的一部药物学巨著，是当时世界上内容最丰富、最详细的药物学文献。《农政全书》是科学家徐光启写的一部农业百科全书。它记载了中国古代有关农业的理论，并总结了中国的农田水利技术，还首次介绍了西方

徐光启像

的农业科学知识。徐光启不但知识广博，而且善于学习外来的先进科学知识。他和意大利传教士利玛窦(mǎ)①一起翻译了西方数学著作《几何原本》，这是中国历史上第一部科技译著。《天工开物》是宋应星编写的，专门介绍了明代农业、手工业的生产技术：如采煤、打井的技术和纺织业使用的提花织机等。书中有大量的插图，人们可以清楚地看到明朝手工工场生产的情景，因此，这本书被称为"中国17世纪的工艺百科全书"。

烧瓷（选自《天工开物》）

明代是中国古典小说蓬勃发展的时期。明朝产生了许多优秀的小说，最著名的长篇小说有《三国演义》《水浒(hǔ)传》和《西游记》等。当时还出现了反对封建礼教的思想家李贽(zhì)。

明朝是一个经济繁荣，对外关系比较开放的国家。它和欧洲的文艺复兴处于同一时

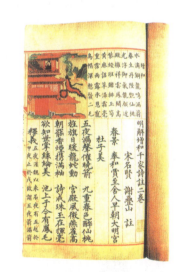

中国最早的彩印插图书（明）

---

① 利玛窦（1552—1610）——意大利人，耶稣会教士，1582年到中国传教。他将西方的科学知识和文化传到中国，又将中国的经典"四书"、"五经"、《道德经》等译成拉丁文，介绍到欧洲。

期。明代前期，远比西方发达。而西方到了文艺复兴以后，才赶上并超过了中国。从此，中国开始渐渐地落后了。

生词

tài jiān 太监	eunuch	xiāo shòu 销售	sell
zhèng 郑	Zheng (surname)	shùn chā 顺差	surplus
bù jú 布局	layout	wén xiàn 文献	document
jīn bì huī huáng 金碧辉煌	resplendent and magnificent	xú guāng qǐ 徐光启	Xu Guangqi (name)
jiā yù guān 嘉峪关	Jiayu Pass	chuán jiào shì 传教士	missionary
duō yú 多余	spare	cǎi méi 采煤	coal mining
gù yōng 雇佣	employment	gōng yì 工艺	craft; technology
yáo 窑	kiln	wén yì fù xīng 文艺复兴	High Renaissance
chéng zhèn 城镇	cities and towns		

听写

徐光启　城镇　销售　采煤　郑成功　多余　金碧辉煌

领先　沿途　胸怀大志　*广博

比一比

领 { 领袖 / 领导 / 带领

献 { 文献 / 献出

城 { 城镇 / 城市

胸 { 胸怀大志 / 胸有成竹

精 { 精巧 / 精美

顺 { 顺差 / 顺利

余 { 多余 / 剩余

{ 煤（采煤） / 谋（谋略）

字词运用

领先

比赛一开始红队领先，后来蓝队超过红队，夺取了冠军。

多余

我们是十个人，您给了十一双鞋，多余一双，请您收回去吧。

沿途

我骑着自行车在郊外旅行，沿途的风景很美丽，我的心情也很愉快。

回答问题

1. 明朝的三部科学巨著名字是什么？请分别说一说它们属于哪一个学科，作者是谁。

2. 你知道明朝哪三部著名的长篇小说？请说一说它们的作者是谁。

词语解释

胸怀大志——心里存着远大的志向。

严整——严格，工整。

金碧辉煌——形容建筑物异常华丽，光彩夺目。

浩大——（声势、规模等）巨大。

精巧——（技术、器物构造等）精细、巧妙。

精美——精巧、漂亮。

沿途——沿路。

花色繁多——花纹和颜色的品种很多。

领先——共同前进时走在最前面。比喻水平、成绩等处于最前列。

广博——范围大，方面多（多指学识）。

封建礼教——使人们的思想和行为符合封建传统的礼节和道德。

阅读

郑和下西洋

郑和像

公元1405年农历六月的一天，太平洋上风平浪静。江苏刘家河水面上却是一片喧闹，这里整齐地排列着62条巨型海船。只听一声令下，十几里长的船队浩浩荡荡，扬帆南下。带领这只船队的是三宝太监郑和。

明朝前期的"与民休息"政策使经济快速增长，中国成了亚洲最富强的国家。当时，中国的纺织、陶瓷制造、造船、航海业都处于世界领先的地位。明成祖是一位思想比较开放的皇帝，他派太监郑和率船队出使西洋各国，提高了中国的威望，促进了国际贸易的往来。

郑和原来姓马，回族人，公元1371年出生在云南。郑和第一次下西洋时，他的船队共有27,000多人，除水手、官兵之外，还有工匠、医生、翻译等。他们的船称为宝船，最大的长约138米，宽56米，可容纳1,000人，是当时世界上最大的海船。船队之大，也是当时世界上独一无二的。公元1492年哥伦布首次远航时，他的船队仅有3艘船（船长18米）和90名水手。

郑和带着国书，每到一国都会和当地的君主会面，宣读国书，赠送珍贵礼物，表示愿意建立友好关系，还热情邀请当地国王访问中国。同时船队也与当地进行贸易活动，用中国的金银、丝绸、瓷器等物品换回珠宝、香料和药材。郑和的远航加强了明朝同各国的友好关系。那时候苏禄等国的国王、王子都来过中国。随郑和前来的使节、商人更是多达上千人。公元1435年，郑和在最后一次出使西洋的归途中死在他乡。郑和是世界历史上最杰出的航海家之一。

郑和七次下西洋，前后28年。他的船队到过亚洲和非洲的30多个国家和地区，最远到达了今天的红海一带和非洲东海岸。直到今天，南洋群岛和印度洋一些地区还保存着纪念郑和的石碑和庙宇。可是，自从郑和死后，中国人的身影就消失在海上了。

生词

xuān nào 喧闹	noise and excitemert		sū lù 苏禄	Sulu
yáng fān 扬帆	set sail		tā xiāng 他乡	alien land
róng nà 容纳	have a capacity of		hóng hǎi 红海	the Red Sea
gē lún bù 哥伦布	Christopher Columbus		miào yǔ 庙宇	temple
guó shū 国书	letter of credence		shēn yǐng 身影	figure
zèng sòng 赠送	present			

 English Translation

Lesson 16

Ming(Ⅰ)

Zhu Yuanzhang, the first emperor of the Ming Dynasty, was born in a poor family and used to be a monk. He then joined the Red-Turban Rebelling at the end of the Yuan Dynasty and became a leader. He founded the Ming Dynasty in 1368AD in today's Nanjing and became Emperor Taizu of the Ming Dynasty.

After the founding of the Ming Dynasty, Zhu Yuanzhang sent his sons to be seigniors in different places and they all led their own armies, among which the one led by Zhu Di in Yan was the strongest. Before his death, Zhu Yuanzhang passed his throne to his grandson Emperor Jianwen. Since Emperor Jianwen was very young at the time, Zhu Di the seignior of Yan rebelled and in 1402AD came to the throne himself by driving away Emperor Jianwen. He then moved the capital from Nanjing to Beijing.

Zhu Di was an ambitious emperor and the Ming Dynasty became increasingly powerful under his rule. He used to send Zheng He and a fleet, a eunuch, on diplomatic missions to the west. The navigation of Zheng He not only improved the reputation of the Ming government, but also promoted the cultural exchanges between China and the west, initiated the interest of Chinese in oversea development. Since then, more and more people immigrated from Guangdong and Fujian to Southeast Asia.

Serving as the capital city of Ming, Beijing has been the political, economic, and cultural center of China for several hundred years. The architecture of Beijing city was neatly arranged, with grand city walls, wide and straight streets, was the masterpiece of city construction in ancient time. The entire city centered on the resplendent and magnificent imperial palace. It is the largest and the best preserved ancient palace complex in the world. The Ming government renovated the Great Wall from Shanhai Pass in the east to Jiayu Pass in the west with a total length of over 6,000 kilometers, making it a huge project.

The policy adopted in the early Ming Dynasty was to reduce the tas, recover and develop the production. Soon, the agricultural output exceeded far beyond the previous dynasties. The input of spare rural labors contributed to the rapid growth of handicraft industry and business. During that time, the handicraft techniques were extremely exquisite, production scale continuously expanded, and there appeared employment relationship. For example, the blue and white porcelain produced during the Ming Dynasty was extremely famous in the world. As for Jingde Town dedicating to the production of porcelain, there were furnaces everywhere within the area of dozens of *li* and tens of hundreds of employees; vehicles and boats loaded with porcelain products could be found everywhere on roads and in rivers passing through the town. The silk products at that time were extremely rich in varieties. After the Mid-Ming Dynasty, the silk textile industry developed in Suzhou and Hangzhou; almost all residents, regardless of sex and age, went for silk textile; rich people were employers and hired both long-term and short-term laborers. There were dozens of weaving machines in large workshops. Exquisite porcelain and silk products were the main commodities that China exported to Europe and America for a large amount of silver. At that time, the Ming government enjoyed favorable balance from international trade.

During the Ming Dynasty, traditional Chinese sciences and technologies still led in the world. The Ming scientists produced three important scientific works: *Compendium of Materia Medica* (Bencao Gangmu), *Complete Treatise on Agricultural Administration* (Nongzheng Quanshu), and *Exploitation of the Works of Nature* (Tiangong Kaiwu). *Compendium of Materia Medica* is a great book on pharmacology written by famous pharmacologist and medical scientist Li Shizhen by summarizing his 27-year experience in the field, was a pharmacological literature with the richest and the most detailed content on pharmacology in the world at that time. *Complete Treatise on Agricultural Administration* is an agricultural encyclopedia written by scientist Xu Guangqi, which records ancient Chinese theories on agriculture, summarizes Chinese water conservancy technologies for farming, and introduced for the first time the western scientific agricultural knowledge. Xu Guangqi was knowledgeable and good at learning from the advanced foreign sciences. He cooperated with Matteo Ricci, an Italian Jesuit Missionary, in the translation of western mathematics literature of Euclid's *Elements*, which is the first translation work on science and technology. *Exploitation of the Works of Nature* written by Song Yingxing, focuses on production technologies on agriculture and handicraft industry during the Ming Dynasty, such as those on coal mining, well digging, and the jacquard loom used in textile industry. There are a large amount of illustrations in his book so that readers can have a better understanding of the production scenes in these workshops of Ming. Accordingly, the book has been famed as the Encyclopedia on Technologies of China in the 17th century.

Chinese classical novels flourished during the Ming Dynasty and there were a lot of masterpieces during the period, including *The Romance of Three Kingdoms*, *Outlaws of the Marsh*, and *Journey to the West*. There was a famous thinker Li Zhi at that time who was against feudal ethical codes.

In general, China enjoyed prosperous economy and relatively open foreign relationship during the Ming Dynasty. This was also the period when Renaissance flourished in Europe. In the early Ming Dynasty, China was much more developed than the west; but after Renaissance, the west caught up with and then overran China. From then on, China began to decline gradually.

Zheng He's Expedition to the West

On day in July 1405AD, the Pacific Ocean was peaceful. But it was boisterous on Liujiahe River of Jiangsu, for 62 massive sea boats were neatly arranged here; at an order, the fleet of a dozen *li* long set sail and headed to south. The one led the fleet was Zheng He, Eunuch Sanbao.

The policy of rehabilitation adopted in the early Ming Dynasty, national economy grew rapidly and China became the most powerful country in Asia. At that time, China led in the world in textile, porcelain production, shipbuilding, and navigation. Emperor Chengzu of the Ming Dynasty was open-minded and sent a fleet led by Zheng He on a diplomatic mission to the west in order to promote the reputation of China and international business and exchanges.

The original surname of Zheng He was Ma, and he was of Hui nationality, born in 1371AD in Yunnan. During the first expedition to the west, his fleet had more than 27,000 men, including sailors, officials, soldiers, craftsmen, doctors, and interpreters. Their boats were known as Treasure Ship; the largest one was 138 meters long and 56 meters wide, capable of holding 1,000 persons, was the largest sea boat in the world at that time and the fleet was also the largest one in the world. In 1492AD when Columbus started his first journey, he merely led a fleet of three boats (18 meters long) and 90 sailors.

Zheng He brought along letters of credence with him and met local monarch when his fleet arrived in each country. He would then read out the letter of credence, presented precious gifts to show the intention of making good relationship with these countries, and invited local monarch to visit China. At the same time, his fleet also did business with local people, changing jewelries, spices, and herbs with gold, silver, silk, and porcelain. The expedition of Zheng He reinforced the friend relationship between the Ming government with other countries. At that time, the kings and princes of Sulu and other countries paid visits to China and more than 1,000 envoys and businessmen came to China along with Zheng He. In 1435AD, Zheng He died in a foreign country on his way back home from the last mission from the west; he was one of the most outstanding navigators in the history of world.

Zheng He has been to the west for seven times in 28 years and his fleet traveled to more than 30 countries and areas in Asia and Africa, reaching as far as today's Red Sea and east coast of Africa. As of today, there are still stone monuments and temples commemorating Zheng He in some places of Southeast Asian islands and Indian Ocean. But after the death of Zheng He, no Chinese could be found on the vast sea.

第十七课

明（下）

明朝的灭亡

明朝中后期，宦官专权，政治腐败。皇亲国戚占有大量土地和财富。农民们失去土地和房屋，缺少衣服和食物，成为"流民"。那个时期，全国的流民多达几百万人。公元1627年，陕西农民的起义爆发了。公元1636年，起义军的一个首领李自成，被众人推举为"闯王"，成为起义军的领袖。当时起义军面临官军的镇压，处境艰难。但是李自成坚持斗争，队伍迅速发展壮大。他还提出了"均田免粮"的口号，得到广大农民的拥

明朝皇后凤冠

《铁冠图》（清末年画——崇祯赐死皇后，然后自杀）

护，起义军很快发展到数十万人。李自成于公元1643年建立大顺朝。公元1644年，李自成带领起义军攻入北京，明朝皇帝在煤山（今北京景山）自杀，明朝灭亡。

李自成进入北京之后，明朝大将吴三桂投降清军，联合清军一起攻打起义军。李自成在山海关被打败，匆忙退出北京城。清军紧追不舍，李自成最后战死于湖北。李自成从进入北京到撤离，前后仅仅41天。

清军占领北京以后，把首都迁到北京，开始了对全国的统治。

民族英雄郑成功

郑成功是抗清名将，也是收复台湾的民族英雄。开始，郑成功以厦门为根据地，起兵抗清。他的队伍不断壮大，曾率领十万

郑成功收复台湾

大军进攻南京。北伐失败以后,他的军队退回到厦门,准备驱逐荷兰人,收复台湾,以台湾为抗清的基地。公元1661年郑成功带领2.5万名将士和数百艘战船,向台湾进军。经过八个月的战斗,于公元1662年打败荷兰人,收复了台湾。

郑成功收复台湾后,下令让几万士兵和随军家属开荒种田。不久,在台湾南部和西部的彰化、新竹等地逐渐形成了一大批村镇。

收复台湾不久,郑成功因病身亡,年仅38岁。他的儿子郑经,孙子郑克塽(shuǎng)前后治理台湾22年。郑氏祖孙三代治理台湾时,奖励制糖、制盐,兴办工商业,发展贸易,开办学堂,改进高山族的农业生产方式。这些都推动了台湾经济、文化的发展。在台湾历史上,这是一个重要的开发和发展时期,史称"明郑时代"。

公元1683年,清政府派军进攻台湾,郑克塽率众归顺。自此台湾在清政府直接统治之下,属福建省。

十色纸(明朝纸的颜色丰富,多用植物染料染色)

生词

huàn guān 宦官	eunuch	qū zhú 驱逐	drive out
huáng qīn guó qì 皇亲国戚	imperial family and their relatives	hé lán 荷兰	Netherland
cái fù 财富	fortune	jī dì 基地	base
chǔ jìng 处境	situation	jiā shǔ 家属	family dependents
zhuàng dà 壮大	strengthen	zhāng huà 彰化	Zhanghua (place)
cōng máng 匆忙	in a hurry	zhì lǐ 治理	govern
shōu fù 收复	recover	guī shùn 归顺	come over and pledge allegiance
xià mén 厦门	Xiamen (place)		

听写

厦门　亲戚　壮大　家属　荷兰　财富　匆忙

收复　基地　*驱逐　处境

比一比

- 宦（宦官）
- 臣（大臣）

- 荷（荷兰）
- 何（如何）

- 厦（厦门）
- 夏（夏天）

- 彰（彰化）
- 章（文章）

- 驱（驱逐）
- 区（区别）

- 财（财富）
- 才（人才）

- 匆（匆忙）
- 勿（请勿入内）

字词运用

匆（匆）忙（忙）

郑先生的时间总是不够用，干什么都是匆匆忙忙的。

近义词

收复——夺回   投降——归顺   宦官——太监

回答问题

1. 明末农民起义的杰出领袖是谁？

2. 郑成功从哪国人的手中收复了台湾？

3. 郑成功哪一年收复了台湾？

词语解释

紧追不舍 —— 紧紧追赶，不肯放弃。

阅读

利玛窦(mǎ)

16世纪新航路开辟后，欧洲的一些天主教传教士来中国传教，其中最有名的是利玛窦。

利玛窦（1552—1610）是意大利人，耶稣会教士，1582年到中国传教。他努力学习汉语，了解中国的风土人情，一两年以后，便可以阅读中国经典了。1585年，他建立了中国内地的第一座天主教堂。

利玛窦很有学问，他精通"四书五经"，尊重中国文化，允许教徒祭孔祭祖，因而得到了中国人的信任和友谊。后来，明朝皇帝接见了他，特许他在北京建教堂传教。那时中国人对天主教很陌生，传教并不容易。他不但向中国人介绍西方的宗教和伦理学，还将西方的科学技术与发明：如欧几里得几何学、三角学、天文

利玛窦像

学、地理学、测量学、透视学、西方乐器等新鲜事物介绍给中国人。

利玛窦在中国20多年，不仅把西方介绍给中国，同时他又把中国的经典"四书"、"五经"、《道德经》等译成拉丁文，介绍到欧洲，成为第一个把孔子和儒家思想介绍给西方的人。利玛窦在中国与西方文化交流的历史上书写了重要的一章。1610年，利玛窦病逝，葬于北京。

生词

yē sū 耶稣	Jesus		jǐ hé xué 几何学	geometry
jì 祭	cult; worship		sān jiǎo xué 三角学	trigonometry
yǒu yì 友谊	friendship		tòu shì xué 透视学	fluoroscopy
mò shēng 陌生	unfamiliar		lā dīng wén 拉丁文	Latin
lún lǐ xué 伦理学	ethnics		bìng shì 病逝	die of illness

Lesson 17

Ming(II)

The End of the Ming Dynasty

In the middle and late Ming Dynasty, eunuchs controlled the power and corruption plagued national politics. Imperial family and their relatives held a large amount of land and fortune, while farmers lost their farming land and houses, were in want of clothes and foods, becoming refugees. At that time, there were several millions of refugees in China. In 1627AD, farmers of Shaanxi started an uprising and in 1636AD, a leader named Li Zicheng was selected to be Chuangwang, the Daring King and their supreme leader. Facing official oppression and difficult situation, he insisted on fighting back and his force grew rapidly. He also proposed to "divide farming land on an equal basis and exempt from tax in the form of grain", which made him extremely popular among farmers. His army quickly grew to several hundred thousand soldiers and Li Zicheng founded the great Shun Dynasty in 1643AD. In 1644AD, Li Zicheng led his army and seized Beijing, the emperor of the Ming Dynasty committed suicide in Coal Hill (today's Jingshan Hill in Beijing), marking the end of the Ming Dynasty.

After Li Zicheng seized Beijing, General Wu Sangui of the Ming Dynasty surrendered to Qing and joined hands with Qing army in fighting with Li Zicheng, who was defeated in Shanhai Pass and retreated from Beijing. With Qing army pursuing behind, Li Zicheng died in a battle in Hubei and he had ruled Beijing for only 41 days.

The Qing army seized Beijing and moved its capital to this city, starting its reign on China.

Zheng Chenggong, a National Hero

Zheng Chenggong is a famous general fighting against the Qing army and a national hero recovering Taiwan. Firstly, Zheng Chenggong was based on Xiamen in fighting against Qing. Along with the growth of his military force, he once led 100,000 soldiers attacking Nanjing. After the failure of north expedition, he retreated to Xiamen, preparing for driving out the Netherlanders and recovering Taiwan so as to continuously fight with Qing based on Taiwan. In 1661AD, Zheng Chenggong led 25,000 soldiers and hundreds of warship marching toward Taiwan. After eight months of fighting, he finally recovered Taiwan in 1662AD by defeating the Netherlanders.

After successfully recovering Taiwan, Zheng Chenggong ordered his tens of thousands soldiers and their dependants to open up and cultivate wasteland. Soon, a large amount of villages and towns appeared in southern and western part of Taiwan including Zhanghua and Xinzhu.

Shortly after recovering Taiwan, Zheng Chenggong died of illness at the age of 38. His son Zheng Jing and grandson Zheng Keshuang have governed Taiwan for 22 years. Under the reign of three generations of Zhengs in Taiwan, they encouraged sugar and salt production industry, promoted industries and business, developed trades, built schools and improved the agricultural production methods of local Gaoshan nationality, which contributed to the development of both economy and culture in Taiwan. In the history of Taiwan, this is an important period of development and growth and known as the period of Zheng regime during the Ming Dynasty.

In 1683AD, the Qing government sent army to attack Taiwan and Zheng Keshuang surrendered; since then, Taiwan was under the direct control of the Qing government and under the administration of Fujian Province.

Matteo Ricci

After the development of new navigation route in the 16th century, many European catholic missionaries came to China and Matteo Ricci was probably the most famous one among them.

Matteo Ricci (1552-1610) was an Italian Jesuit Missionary and arrived in China in 1582AD. He worked hard to learn Chinese and to understand Chinese customs, was able to read Chinese classics one or two years later. In 1585AD, he built the first Catholic Church in inland China.

Matteo Ricci was learned and an expert on *Four Books* and *Five Classics*; he respected Chinese culture and allowed believers to worship Confucius and ancestors, gaining accordingly trust and friendship of Chinese people. Later, the emperor of the Ming Dynasty sent for him and allowed him to build church and missionize in Beijing. At that time, Catholicism was strange to Chinese and it was not an easy task to missionize them. He introduced to Chinese people not only western religion and ethnics, but also western scientific and technologic achievements including Euclid's geometry, trigonometry, astronomy, geography, surveying, fluoroscopy, as well as new things such as western instruments.

During his 20 years stay in China, apart from introducing the western world to China, Matteo Ricci also translated into Latin and introduced to Europe Chinese classic literature including *Four Books*, *Five Classics*, and *Tao Teh Ching* of Laozi, making him the first one introducing Confucius and Confucianism to the west. Matteo Ricci composed an important chapter in the history of cultural communication between China and the west. In 1610AD, Matteo Ricci died of illness and was buried in Beijing.

第十八课

清（上）

清朝是中国封建社会最后一个朝代，是由满族人建立的。满族在历史上称为女真，居住在黑龙江下游。公元1616年，努尔哈赤统一了女真部落，建立金政权（史称后金）。公元1636年，努尔哈赤的儿子皇太极改国号为"清"。公元1644年，李自成领导的农民起义军推翻了明朝，清军乘机进入山海关，打败了起义军，定都北京。

康熙皇帝像

清朝初期实行奖励开荒，减少税收的政策，内地和边疆经济都有了发展。到18世纪中叶，清的国力强大起来，人口达3亿多。

康熙皇帝是中国历史上一位有名的皇帝。公元1683年，他出兵统一了台湾，在台湾设一府三县，属福建省。清军占领全中国，先后用了几十年时间。在这期间，俄罗斯多次进犯中国黑龙江地区，并占领雅克萨城。康熙皇帝两次派兵出击，俄军战败。1689年，两国签订《尼布楚条约》，划定边界，从此以后的一百多年里，中国东北十分平静。到乾隆皇帝（康熙帝的孙子）时，最终平定了蒙古准噶尔部，统一了新疆。之后，清政府注意发展边疆的经济、文化和交通，巩固了中国多民族国家的统一，清朝的疆域达到1,200万平方千米。

故宫乾清宫

雍(yōng)正皇帝（康熙帝的儿子）时，改革了税收制度，取消了丁银（人头税），只按土地收税，减轻了人民的负担，农业生产得到发展。

早在明朝时，中国与西方国家之间，不仅商贸活动频繁，而且文化交流也有所增加。1582年，意大利传教士利玛窦等已来到中国传教。后来，日耳曼人汤若望等陆续来华。传教士来

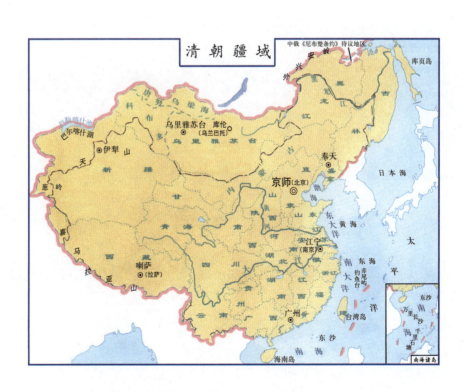

到中国，带来了西方的科学知识，比如数学、天文学、地理学。

《万国来朝图》局部（清）

同时，传教士本身也学习中国的儒学、佛学。不过，罗马教皇禁止中国教徒祭孔祭祖，这触及到中国传统文化的根本，因此，清朝时康熙皇帝下令禁止中国人信天主教。

从康熙到乾隆三代，国家稳定，社会繁荣，被称为"康乾盛世"。但是，大清国以天朝上国自居，并未觉察世界的另一边正发生着翻天覆地的巨大变化。欧洲人通过远洋航行开辟了海外市场，商业经济快速取代了农业经济；欧洲的工业革命带来了全新的生产方式和巨大的社会变化；科学实证代替了神学教条；民主、法制、契约的思想和制度代替了专制王权的思想和制度，法国、美国建立了民主政权，人民开始用选票治理自己的国家。这一切是那么新鲜而有活力，西方国家正大步前进。而大清国，在经济上依然是以农业立国，文化上提倡封建礼教，甚至大兴"文字狱"①。清政府这种闭关自守、盲目自大、不思进取的做法，致使中国落后于世界的先进潮流。

---

① 文字狱——统治者故意从诗文中摘取字句制造罪名，迫害知识分子。

第十八课

生词

chéng jī 乘机	seize the opportunity		chù jí 触及	touch
kāng xī 康熙	Emperor Kangxi		zì jū 自居	claim oneself to be
qiān dìng 签订	sign		jué chá 觉察	perceive
huà dìng 划定	delimit; demarcate		mín zhǔ 民主	democracy
qián lóng 乾隆	Emperor Qianlong		qì yuē 契约	contract
zhǔn gá ěr 准噶尔	Junggar		zhuān zhì 专制	autocratic
fù dān 负担	burden		yǐ zhì （以）致	as a result
rì ěr màn 日耳曼	Teutonic; German		cháo liú 潮流	current; tide
jì kǒng 祭孔	worship Confucius			

听写

乘机　签订　负担　觉察　民主　（以）致　法制

日耳曼　自大　潮流　*翻天覆地　祭孔

比一比

乘 { 乘机 / 乘法 }　　签 { 签订 / 签字 }　　覆 { 翻天覆地 / 覆盖 }　　{ 祭(祭孔) / 际(国际) }

负 { 负担 / 负责 }　　觉 { 觉察 / 觉得 }　　盲 { 盲目 / 盲人 }　　{ 致(以致) / 至(甚至) }

字词运用

自大

骄傲自大的人往往会失败。

负担

做作业是为了巩固课堂学习的知识，但是作业不能太多，否则学生负担太重。

回答问题

1. 清朝是由哪一个民族建立的？它是中国封建社会最后一个朝代吗？

2. 清朝时，中国为什么落后于世界先进的潮流？

词语解释

教徒——信仰某种宗教的人。

翻天覆地——形容变化巨大，而且是根本的改变。

实证——实际的证明。

神学教条——宗教上的信条，信徒只能相信、服从，不能批评、怀疑。

闭关自守——闭塞关口，不跟外界往来。

盲目自大——毫无根据地自以为了不起，看不起别人。

不思进取——没有进步的愿望。

阅读

四库全书

清朝的文化思想,一方面提倡儒家礼教,打压一切反清言行和文字,另一方面,康乾时期,由官方组织大批学者编写了《四库全书》和《康熙字典》等许多书籍。

《四库全书》由乾隆皇帝亲自主持,于1773年在北京开始编写,光是参加编写的学者就多达500人,再加上抄写者,共计3,800人。

编写《四库全书》的学者和官员们,首先在全国收集各种珍藏书籍,然后又细心整理和恢复了500多种珍贵文献。经过十年的努力,全书共收集了3,400多种,79,000多卷,36,304册书,为后人保留了许多珍贵的书籍和资料。《四库全书》是封建社会官方修订的最大丛书。

《四库全书》编成后,抄成七份,分别藏于北京故宫和江浙等地的藏书楼中。其中,江浙的藏书楼对公众开放,供各地文人查阅。

文津阁中的《四库全书》

清末和民国初期，由于连年战火，《四库全书》大部分遗失，留存本现存在台湾和北京图书馆。

《四库全书》的编写，虽有保存珍贵文献的作用，但也是一次文化清查。一些所谓的反清书籍被销毁了，数量达2,400多种。

珐琅彩双联瓶（清）

生词

guān fāng 官方	by the government; offcial	yí shī 遗失	lose
cè 册	volume	liú cún běn 留存本	the remain books
xiū dìng 修订	revise	wén huà qīng chá 文化清查	a thorough inspection on cultural heritages
cóng shū 丛书	series		
gōng zhòng 公众	general public	xiāo huǐ 销毁	destroy by burning

Lesson 18

Qing (I)

The Qing Dynasty is the last feudal dynasty in the history of China and was founded by Man nationality, who was known as Nuzhen in the history and lived in the lower reaches of Heilongjiang River. Nurhachi unified the entire Nuzhen tribe in 1616AD and founded the regime of Jin (known as Later Jin in the history). In 1636AD, Huangtaiji, a son of Nurhachi, changed the name into Qing. In 1644AD, Li Zicheng led uprising farmers and overthrew the Ming government; the Qing army took the opportunity by going beyond the Shanhai Pass and defeating Li Zicheng, finally seized the capital city of Beijing.

In the early Qing Dynasty, the government encouraged people to open up wasteland by cutting taxes, resulting in the economic growth in both inland and border areas. In the middle 18th century, China became strong with a total population of more than 300 million.

Emperor Kangxi is a famous emperor in the history of China; in 1683AD, he unified Taiwan and established one government office and three counties in Taiwan under the administration of Fujian Province. It took the Qing government a couple of dozens of years to take hold of the entire China and during this period of time, Russia invaded Heilongjiang area several times and took over Yakesa city. Emperor Kangxi sent army to fight with Russians twice and finally defeated them. In 1689AD, two countries signed *Nerchinsk Treaty* to clarify borders and China won peace in its northwest area for more than 100 years after that. Under the reign of Emperor Qianlong (the grandson of Emperor Kangxi), Xinjiang was unified by controlling Mongolian Junggar tribe; then the Qing government emphasized the development of economy, culture and communication in border areas, consolidating the unification of this country of multiple nationalities. The total area of the territory during the Qing Dynasty was 12 million square kilometers.

Emperor Yongzheng (the son of Emperor Kangxi) reformed taxation system and cancelled silver levied on the person (poll tax), collecting land-based tax and reducing the burden on people, resulting in the growth of agricultural production.

As early as during the Ming Dynasty, business activities between China and the western countries were active and cultural exchanges also grew considerably. In 1582, Italian missionaries including famous Matteo Ricci came to China to missionize people here and they were later followed by Johann Adam Schall von Bell, a German missionary. These missionaries came to China and brought with them the western scientific knowledge on mathematics, astronomy, and geography. Meanwhile, they also learned Chinese Confucianism and Buddhism. But since the Pope forbid Chinese believers to worship Confucius and ancestors, which violated the root of traditional Chinese culture, therefore Emperor Kangxi of the Qing Dynasty ordered that no Chinese was allowed to believe in Catholicism.

Under the reign of three emperors from Kangxi to Qianlong, China enjoyed stability and prosperity, and the period was known in the history a Golden Age of Kang-Qian. But since the Qing government considered China a celestial empire and was unaware of the tremendous and revolutionary changes undergone on the other side of the world. Europeans developed oversea markets through sea routes and quickly replaced agricultural economy with commercial economy, while European Industrial Revolution brought long brand new production method and huge social changes. Scientific demonstration replaced theological doctrine. Democracy, legal system as well as concept and system of contract replaced absolute monarchy, democratic system was established in both France and US, where people started to govern their own country through the means of voting. All these were innovative and energetic, and the western countries progressed greatly. On the contrary, under the reign of the Qing government, Chinese economy still mainly depended on agriculture; it advocated feudal ethical codes and literary inquisition was strict at that time. The Qing government shut China from any communication with other countries, was arrogant blindly, and refused to make any changes and progresses, which resulted in the lagging of China behind other countries.

Complete Library in Four Branches of Literature

As for the culture and ideology during the Qing Dynasty, on the one hand, the government advocated Confucian ethical codes and oppressed all activities and literature works against Qing; on the other hand, under the reign of Emperor Kangxi and Qianlong, the official organized a large amount of scholars in composing a series of books, including *Complete Library in Four Branches of Literature* (Siku Quanshu) and *Kangxi Dictionary* (Kangxi Zidian).

Emperor Qianlong was in charge of the composition of *Complete Library in Four Branches of Literature* himself, and the project started in Beijing in 1773AD, some 500 scholars participated in the project, together with copyists, a total of 3,800 people were involved in the project.

To start with, the scholars and officials composing *Complete Library in Four Branches of Literature* collected carefully preserved books in the entire country and then filed and restored more than 500 precious literatures. After a decade of efforts, the library collected 3,400 books, 79,000 chapters and 36,304 volumes, leaving to descendants a lot of precious books and materials. It is the largest series edited by the feudal authority.

After the accomplishment of its composition, seven copies of *Complete Library in Four Branches of Literature* were transcribed and stored separately in libraries located in the Palace Museum of Beijing, Jiangsu and Zhejiang, among which these in Jiangsu and Zhejiang were open to the public for the reference of local scholars.

At the end of the Qing Dynasty and the early Republic of China, due to continuous wars, most copies of *Complete Library in Four Branches of Literature* were lost and the existing ones are now kept in Taiwan and Beijing Library.

The composition of *Complete Library in Four Branches of Literature* served the function of preserving precious literature, but on the other hand, it was also a thorough inspection on cultural heritages, during which many books supposed with content against the Qing government were destroyed and the total kind of these books reached 2,400.

第十九课

清（下）

18世纪末，在中英贸易中，英国一直有很大的逆差。爱喝茶的英国人每年从中国进口大量茶叶，而英国的呢绒、钟表等在中国却销路不好。为此，英国曾派使节访华，想以外交手段打开中国市场，但是被乾隆皇帝拒绝了。为了改变贸易逆差，英国居然冒天下之大不韪(wěi)，开始了罪恶的鸦片贸易。到了公元1838年，每年有4万多箱鸦片卖到中国，不但老百姓深受其害，而且白银大量外流。从公元1820年到1840年，从中国流出的白银相当于当时大清国两年的财政总收入。

林则徐像

公元1838年底，清朝皇帝命令林则徐禁烟。第二年，林则徐到达广州之后，

鸦片战争海战图

在虎门将收缴的鸦片全部销毁，这就是历史上著名的"虎门销烟"。公元1840年，英国派军舰入侵中国广州和浙江，发动了"鸦片战争"，受到清军奋力抵抗，英军败退。可是英国人转而北上，

到达天津，直逼北京。后来英军又深入长江口，打到南京城下。公元1842年，清政府被迫同英国签订了中国近代史上第一个不平等条约——中英《南京条约》。条约规定：中国向英国赔偿2,100万银圆，割让香港岛，开放五个通商口岸，以及英国单方面拥有"领事裁判权"①等。从此，中国沦为半殖民地半封建社会。

鸦片战争以后，英国、法国在公元1856年又发动了第二次鸦片战争，企图得到更多的利益。公元1860年英法联军攻进北京，放火烧毁了举世无双的皇家园林——圆明园，清朝咸丰皇帝逃到承德。公元1861年，咸丰皇帝病死，他的贵妃联合他的一个弟弟发动了北京政变，掌握了政权，这个贵妃就是后来的慈禧(xǐ)太后，也称"西太后"。西太后统治的时期是清朝最黑暗和衰落的时期。她顽固守旧，反对革新。她镇压太平天国农民起义②、义和团运动③，并杀

圆明园大水法遗迹

---

① 领事裁判权——英国人在中国犯了罪，中国法庭无权审判，只能由本国的领事来裁判。

② 太平天国农民起义——公元1851年，洪秀全领导农民起义，建立太平天国。

③ 义和团运动——19世纪末，中国北方的农民和城市平民自发组织的反对帝国主义的武装斗争。

圆明园大水法（喷泉）

害了百日维新①的英雄谭嗣(sì)同等人；对英、法、日等国的侵略却无力抵抗，节节败退。

19世纪后半期的五十年中，鸦片贸易成了合法贸易。外国的入侵规模一次比一次大，对中国造成的伤害一次比一次严重。开始是俄国强迫清政府签订了《瑷珲(ài huī)条约》，以后又有中法战争和《中法新约》，中日甲午战争和《马关条约》，八国联军②侵华战争和《辛丑条约》等等。这些条约使中国丧失了东北和西北的150万平方千米的土地和台湾、香港新界、大连、青岛等地方，赔款总计十几亿两白银（包括利息）。中国遭受了前所未有的打击，老百姓再也不能忍受下去，一场浩大的革命开始了，革命的领导者是孙中山。

---

① 百日维新——又称戊(wù xū)戌变法，是公元1898年光绪皇帝支持康有为、梁启超等人进行的一次政治改革，仅仅103天就被慈禧太后镇压下去，变法失败。

② 八国联军——1900年由英、美、德、法、俄、日、意、奥八国组成的侵华联军。

第十九课

孙中山

孙中山（1866—1925），字逸仙，广东香山县（今中山县）人，中国民主革命的伟大先行者和伟大爱国者。他为中国的独立、民主、富强奋斗了一生。孙中山决心推翻清政府，在中国建立一个民主的国家。他首先成立了一个反清革命团体——兴中会。1905年，他又联合其他革命团体，在日本东京创立了中国同盟会，提出了"驱除鞑(dá)虏，恢复中华，建立民国，平均地权"的口号。同盟会成立以后，革命者在长江中下游和南方各地，连续发动了一系列武装起义。经过长期艰苦的努力，1911年10月10日，革命党人在武昌的起义终于取得了成功，各省革命党人和反清力量纷纷响应。因为1911年是中国农历辛亥年，所以这次革命被称为辛亥革命。1912年1月1日，孙中山在南京就任中华民国临时大总统。之后，清朝皇帝宣布退位。但是，后来权力落到了北洋军阀袁世凯的手中。

武昌起义后成立的湖北军政府

辛亥革命推翻了清王朝，结束了中国两千多年的封建君主制度，建立了中华民国。

生词

nì chā 逆差	adverse balance of trade	cái pàn 裁判	judge
ní róng 呢绒	wollen cloth	zhí mín dì 殖民地	colony
jù jué 拒绝	refuse; reject	wán gù 顽固	stubborn
zuì è 罪恶	evil	tán 谭	Tan (surname)
yā piàn 鸦片	opium	xīn hài gé mìng 辛亥革命	the Revolution of 1911
shōu jiǎo 收缴	take over; confiscate	xiǎng yìng 响应	respond
xiāo huǐ 销毁	destroy by burning	lín shí 临时	temporary
jūn jiàn 军舰	warship	kǎi 凯	triumphant
péi cháng 赔偿	compensate		

听写

拒绝　军舰　赔偿　裁判　临时　凯（歌）　顽固　响应

罪恶　殖民地　*逆差　鸦片

比一比

罪 { 罪恶 / 受罪 / 犯罪

响 { 响应 / 影响 / 响声

赔 { 赔偿 / 赔款 / 赔钱

舰（军舰）/ 船（小船）

使 { 使节 / 使用

镇 { 镇压 / 城镇

殖 { 殖民地 / 繁殖

裁 { 裁判 / 裁缝

字词运用

遭受

亲爱的妈妈去世了，他遭受了一次沉重的打击，心情十分悲痛。

忍受

窗外机器的响声吵得大家上不了课，师生们实在忍受不了了。

赔偿

损坏了别人的财物就应该赔偿。

反义词

逆差——顺差   拒绝——接受

多音字

呢 ní   呢 ne

呢 ní 呢绒   呢 ne 在哪儿呢

回答问题

1. 鸦片战争爆发的原因是什么?

2. 为什么说签订《南京条约》使中国变成了半殖民地半封建的国家?

3. 什么革命推翻了清朝?革命的领导人是谁?

词语解释

冒天下之大不韪——做天下人都认为不对的坏事。

举世无双——世界上没有第二个。

合法——符合法律规定。

驱除鞑虏——赶走满清(统治者)。

林则徐虎门销烟

林则徐（1785—1850），福建省福州人，是中国近代的民族英雄。

公元1839年，清道光皇帝派林则徐去广东禁烟。林则徐到达广州后，当众表示"如鸦片一日未禁绝，本大臣一日不回京"。公元1839年3月16日，林则徐下令收缴外商鸦片。他限外商三天内交出所有鸦片；个人还要出保证书，声明：以后来船绝不夹带鸦片。林则徐又在广东省内下令严禁贩卖、吸食鸦片，两个月内捕获贩卖、吸食鸦片者1,600多名，收缴鸦片46万两，烟枪4万多支；收缴外商鸦片2万多箱，合计1,188吨。

虎门销烟（人民英雄纪念碑浮雕）

公元1839年6月3日，林则徐在虎门开始销烟。清兵在虎门海滩高地上，筑了两个长宽各45米的方形大池子，并放入盐水。先把鸦片过秤后投入水中，再将石灰撒入池中，池水顿时沸腾，直到鸦片全部化尽。虎门销烟进行了23天。附近居民欢欣鼓舞，纷纷前往观看这一空前壮举。

林则徐虎门销烟，震惊世界。它向全世界表明了中国人禁烟的决心和反抗外国侵略的坚强意志。

生词

bǎo zhèng shū 保证书	guarantee	zhuàng jǔ 壮举	magnificent feat
jiā dài 夹带	carry secretly	zhèn jīng 震惊	astound
dùn shí 顿时	immediately	jiān qiáng 坚强	strong
fèi téng 沸腾	boil	yì zhì 意志	will
huān xīn gǔ wǔ 欢欣鼓舞	be great overjoyed and inspired		

English Translation

Lesson 19

Qing (II)

At the end of the 18th century, as for Sino-British trade, the United Kingdom suffered great deficit. British people loved drinking tea and had to import a large amount of tea leaves from China, while its woolen goods and clocks were not well marketed. Accordingly, the United Kingdom used to send envoys to China in the hope of developing the Chinese market with diplomatic measures, only to be refused by Emperor Qianlong. In order to reverse the trade deficit, the United Kingdom risked everyone's condemnation and started the villainous opium trade. As form 1838AD, more than 40,000 boxes opium were sold to China every year, doing great damage to ordinary people and resulting in the outflow of a large amount of silver. From 1820AD to 1840AD, the total value of silver flowing out of China equaled to two-year financial revenue of the Qing government.

  At the end of 1838AD, the emperor of the Qing Dynasty ordered Lin Zexu to ban opium smoking and trading. The next year, Lin Zexu arrived at Guangzhou and destroyed all confiscated opium in Humen. This is the famous Destruction of Opium at Humen in the history. In 1840AD, the United Kingdom sent warship to invade Guangzhou and Zhejiang, starting the Opium War. Due to the resistance of the Qing

army, the British army suffered failure there and turned to the north till Tianjin and threatened Beijing. Then the British army went deep through the mouth of the Yangtze River till the Nanjing city. In 1842AD, the Qing government was forced to sign with the United Kingdom *Nanjing Treaty*, the first treaty of inequality in the modern history of China. According to the treaty, China should compensate the United Kingdom 21 million silver dollars, cede Hong Kong Island, open five trading ports, and grant the United Kingdom unilateral consular jurisdiction. Since then, China became semi-colonist and semi-feudal society.

After the Opium War, the United Kingdom and France started the Second Opium War in 1856AD in the hope of getting more interests. In 1860AD, British and French expeditionary forces entered Beijing and set fire on the Winter Palace (Yuan Ming Yuan), the unprecedented imperial park. Emperor Xianfeng of the Qing Dynasty escaped to Chengde and, after his death due to illness in 1861AD, one of his concubines joined hands with one of his brothers in launching a coup d'état in Beijing and successfully seized the ruling power. The concubine was later known as Empress Dowager Cixi or the West Empress Dowager; the period under her reign was the darkest and the most declining stage of the entire Qing Dynasty. She was stubborn, conservative, and strongly against reform. She repressed the farmer uprising of the Taiping Heavenly Kingdom, the Yihetuan Movement, and ordered to kill heroes of 100-Day Reform Movement of 1898 including Tan Sitong. On the contrary, facing the invasion of UK, France and Japan, the Qing government at the time could not resist but retreating.

Within 50 years in late 19th century, opium trade became legal and the scale of foreign invasions grew, causing increasingly severe damages to China. Firstly, Russia forced the Qing government to sign *Treaty of Aigun*; then after the war with France, *Sino-France New Treaty* was signed; after Sino-Japanese war, *Treaty of Shimonoseki*; after the invasion war of Eight Power Allied Force, *Treaty of 1901* was signed. With these treaties of inequality, China lost a total territory of 1.5 million square kilometers in Northeast and Northwest as well as Taiwan, New Territories of Hong Kong, Dalian and Qingdao, and paid a total indemnity of over one billion *liang* of silver (including interest). China suffered the greatest strike in its history and people could no longer stand it. A great revolution was to be initiated, and the leader was Sun Zhongshan (Sun Yat-Sen).

Sun Zhongshan (1866-1925), also known as Yat-Sen, with the alias of Zhongshan, born in Xiangshan County (today's Zhongshan County) of Guangdong, was a great pioneer and patriot of Chinese democratic revolution. He devoted all his life for the independence, democracy, and prosperity of China. Sun Zhongshan determined to overthrow the Qing government and build it into a democratic country. He firstly established Revive China Society, a revolutionary group against Qing. In 1905AD, he cooperated with other revolutionary groups and founded in Tokyo, Japan, Chinese Revolutionary Alliance (Tongmenghui), proposing "to overthrow the Manchu empire and to restore China to the Chinese, to establish a Republic, and to distribute land equally among the people". After the founding of Chinese Revolutionary Alliance, the revolutionists launched a series of armed uprisings in the middle and lower reaches of the Yangtze River and in southern China. Through years of efforts and finally on 10 October 1911, the uprising in Wuchang succeeded, which was responded by revolutionists and forces against the Qing government in other provinces. Since 1911 is the Year of Xinhai (the forty-eighth year in a cycle of sixty years) according to the traditional Chinese lunar calendar, the revolution is then known as the Revolution of Xinhai, or the Revolution of 1911. On 1 January 1912, Sun Zhongshan took the post of interim president of the Republic of China in Nanjing. Then the emperor of the Qing Dynasty announced to abdicate. But later on, the power was seized by Yuan Shikai, a northern warlord.

The Revolution of 1911 overthrew the Qing Dynasty and ended the feudal monarchy in China with a long history of more than 2,000 years by founding the Republic of China.

The Destruction of Opium at Humen Led by Lin Zexu

Lin Zexu (1785-1850) born in Fuzhou, Fujian Province, was a national hero in modern history of China.

In 1839AD, Emperor Daoguang of the Qing Dynasty sent Lin Zexu to Guangdong for banning on opium-smoking and the opium trade. After his arriving in Guangzhou, Lin Zexu announced to the public that "I won't come back to Beijing until opium is banned." On 16 March 1839, Lin Zexu ordered to confiscate opium from foreign businessmen and gave them three-day deadline to hand over all their opium together with personal statement promising not to transport opium on boat in future. Then Lin Zexu distributed orders in Guangdong Province that no opium was allowed to be sold and taken. Within following two months, the local government caught more than 1,600 people selling or taking opium, confiscated 460,000 *liang* of opium and more than 40,000 opium pipes, as well as 20,000 boxes and 1,188 tons of opium from foreign businessmen.

On 3 June 1839, Lin Zexu ordered to destroy all the confiscated opium in Humen. The Qing soldiers dug two square pools of 45 meters long and wide on the highland on the beach of Humen and then filled the pools with salt water. They weighed the opium and then threw into water before spreading lime into the pool, which made the water inside the pools boiling till all opium melt. It took 23 days to destroy all the opium at Humen. The local people were overjoyed and witnessed the grand view in groups.

The Destruction of Opium at Humen led by Lin Zexu shook the world, showing the determination of Chinese people in banning opium and their strong will in fighting against the foreign invaders.

生字表（简）

	péng	bó	shù	chǒng	fēi	nài	cháo	pàn	càn	yǔn	xún
11.	蓬	勃	庶	宠	妃	奈	巢	叛	灿	允	询

	cái	yōng	jiān	qīn	lǔ	guī	xiǔ
12.	财	庸	奸	钦	掳	瑰	朽

	qì	dǎng	fú	zhào	xiáng	fāng	qīn	chāo
13.	契	党	俘	召	祥	芳	侵	钞

	chí	xiōng	xù	wù	kuà	lái	yīn	yī	miǎn	diàn
14.	驰	匈	旭	兀	跨	莱	茵	伊	缅	甸

	hè	jiǎn	péng	kěn	sāng	chàng	yuè	cáo	dìng	dòu	xiāng	qí
15.	赫	检	澎	垦	桑	倡	跃	漕	订	窦	厢	歧

	zhèng	bì	jiā	yù	gù	yōng	yáo	shòu	xú	méi
16.	郑	碧	嘉	峪	雇	佣	窑	售	徐	煤

	huàn	cōng	shà	zhāng
17.	宦	匆	厦	彰

	xī	qián	gá	màn	jì	zhì
18.	熙	乾	噶	曼	祭	致

	nì	róng	jù	jiǎo	jiàn	cháng	pàn	tán	hài	kǎi
19.	逆	绒	拒	缴	舰	偿	判	谭	亥	凯

共计 78 个生字

生字表（繁）

	péng	bó	shù	chǒng	fēi	nài	cháo	pàn	càn	yǔn	xún
11.	蓬	勃	庶	寵	妃	奈	巢	叛	燦	允	詢

	cái	yōng	jiān	qīn	lǔ	guī	xiǔ
12.	財	庸	奸	欽	擄	瑰	朽

	qì	dǎng	fú	zhào	xiáng	fāng	qīn	chāo
13.	契	黨	俘	召	祥	芳	侵	鈔

	chí	xiōng	xù	wù	kuà	lái	yīn	yī	miǎn	diàn
14.	馳	匈	旭	兀	跨	萊	茵	伊	緬	甸

	hè	jiǎn	péng	kěn	sāng	chàng	yuè	cáo	dìng	dòu	xiāng	qí
15.	赫	檢	澎	墾	桑	倡	躍	漕	訂	竇	廂	歧

	zhèng	bì	jiā	yù	gù	yōng	yáo	shòu	xú	méi
16.	鄭	碧	嘉	峪	雇	傭	窯	售	徐	煤

	huàn	cōng	shà	zhāng
17.	宦	匆	廈	彰

	xī	qián	gá	màn	jì	zhì
18.	熙	乾	噶	曼	祭	致

	nì	róng	jù	jiǎo	jiàn	cháng	pàn	tán	hài	kǎi
19.	逆	絨	拒	繳	艦	償	判	譚	亥	凱

共計 78 個生字

生词表（简）

11. 蓬勃（péng bó） 富庶（fù shù） 刺绣（cì xiù） 宠爱（chǒng ài） 贵妃（guì fēi） 愤怒（fèn nù） 无奈（wú nài） 黄巢（huáng cháo）
    叛变（pàn biàn） 灿烂（càn làn） 允许（yǔn xǔ） 宗教（zōng jiào） 子午线（zǐ wǔ xiàn） 询（xún） 风格（fēng gé）

12. 解除（jiě chú） 交纳（jiāo nà） 财政（cái zhèng） 改革（gǎi gé） 低（利）息（dī (lì) xī） 保守派（bǎo shǒu pài） 昏庸（hūn yōng）
    奸臣（jiān chén） 宋钦宗（sòng qīn zōng） 割地（gē dì） 掳走（lǔ zǒu） 瑰宝（guī bǎo） 描绘（miáo huì） 不朽（bù xiǔ）

13. 契丹（qì dān） 维持（wéi chí） 党项（dǎng xiàng） 俘虏（fú lǔ） 北伐（běi fá） 召回（zhào huí） 文天祥（wén tiān xiáng）
    千古流芳（qiān gǔ liú fāng） 从容（cóng róng） 就义（jiù yì） 侵略（qīn lüè） 应用（yìng yòng） 推广（tuī guǎng） 发行（fā xíng）
    钞票（chāo piào）

14. 游牧（yóu mù） 奔驰（bēn chí） 混乱（hùn luàn） 匈牙利（xiōng yá lì） 旭烈兀（xù liè wù） 跨（kuà） 莱茵河（lái yīn hé）
    北冰洋（běi bīng yáng） 伊朗（yī lǎng） 伊拉克（yī lā kè） 土耳其（tǔ ěr qí） 缅甸（miǎn diàn） 巴基斯坦（bā jī sī tǎn）

15. 赫赫武功（hè hè wǔ gōng） 面貌（miàn mào） 检（查）（jiǎn chá） 澎湖列岛（péng hú liè dǎo） 开垦（kāi kěn） 桑（sāng） 提倡（tí chàng）
    活跃（huó yuè） 经历（jīng lì） 漕运（cáo yùn） 制订（zhì dìng） 戏曲（xì qǔ） 窦厢（dòu xiāng） 歧视（qí shì） 领袖（lǐng xiù）

16. 太监（tài jiān） 郑（zhèng） 布局（bù jú） 金碧辉煌（jīn bì huī huáng） 嘉峪关（jiā yù guān） 多余（duō yú） 雇佣（gù yōng）
    窑（yáo） 城镇（chéng zhèn） 销售（xiāo shòu） 顺差（shùn chā） 文献（wén xiàn） 徐光启（xú guāng qǐ） 传教士（chuán jiào shì）
    采煤（cǎi méi） 工艺（gōng yì） 文艺复兴（wén yì fù xīng）

17. 宦官　皇亲国戚　财富　处境　壮大　匆忙　收复
　　厦门　驱逐　荷兰　基地　家属　彰化　治理　归顺

18. 乘机　康熙　签订　划定　乾隆　准噶尔　负担
　　日耳曼　祭孔　触及　自居　觉察　民主　契约　专制
　　（以）致　潮流

19. 逆差　呢绒　拒绝　罪恶　鸦片　收缴　销毁　军舰
　　赔偿　裁判　殖民地　顽固　谭　辛亥革命　响应
　　临时　凯

共计 139 个生词

生词表（繁）

11. 蓬勃 (péng bó)　富庶 (fù shù)　刺綉 (cì xiù)　寵愛 (chǒng ài)　貴妃 (guì fēi)　憤怒 (fèn nù)　無奈 (wú nài)　黃巢 (huáng cháo)
    叛變 (pàn biàn)　燦爛 (càn làn)　允許 (yǔn xǔ)　宗教 (zōng jiào)　子午綫 (zǐ wǔ xiàn)　詢 (xún)　風格 (fēng gé)

12. 解除 (jiě chú)　交納 (jiāo nà)　財政 (cái zhèng)　改革 (gǎi gé)　低（利）息 (dī lì xī)　保守派 (bǎo shǒu pài)　昏庸 (hūn yōng)
    奸臣 (jiān chén)　宋欽宗 (sòng qīn zōng)　割地 (gē dì)　擄走 (lǔ zǒu)　瑰寶 (guī bǎo)　描繪 (miáo huì)　不朽 (bù xiǔ)

13. 契丹 (qì dān)　維持 (wéi chí)　黨項 (dǎng xiàng)　俘虜 (fú lǔ)　北伐 (běi fá)　召回 (zhào huí)　文天祥 (wén tiān xiáng)
    千古流芳 (qiān gǔ liú fāng)　從容 (cóng róng)　就義 (jiù yì)　侵略 (qīn lüè)　應用 (yìng yòng)　推廣 (tuī guǎng)　發行 (fā xíng)
    鈔票 (chāo piào)

14. 游牧 (yóu mù)　奔馳 (bēn chí)　混亂 (hùn luàn)　匈牙利 (xiōng yá lì)　旭烈兀 (xù liè wù)　跨 (kuà)　萊茵河 (lái yīn hé)
    北冰洋 (běi bīng yáng)　伊朗 (yī lǎng)　伊拉克 (yī lā kè)　土耳其 (tǔ ěr qí)　緬甸 (miǎn diàn)　巴基斯坦 (bā jī sī tǎn)

15. 赫赫武功 (hè hè wǔ gōng)　面貌 (miàn mào)　檢（查）(jiǎn chá)　澎湖列島 (péng hú liè dǎo)　開墾 (kāi kěn)　桑 (sāng)　提倡 (tí chàng)
    活躍 (huó yuè)　經歷 (jīng lì)　漕運 (cáo yùn)　制訂 (zhì dìng)　戲曲 (xì qǔ)　竇厢 (dòu xiāng)　歧視 (qí shì)　領袖 (lǐng xiù)

16. 太監 (tài jiān)　鄭 (zhèng)　佈局 (bù jú)　金碧輝煌 (jīn bì huī huáng)　嘉峪關 (jiā yù guān)　多餘 (duō yú)　雇傭 (gù yōng)
    窰 (yáo)　城鎮 (chéng zhèn)　銷售 (xiāo shòu)　順差 (shùn chā)　文獻 (wén xiàn)　徐光啟 (xú guāng qǐ)　傳教士 (chuán jiào shì)
    採煤 (cǎi méi)　工藝 (gōng yì)　文藝復興 (wén yì fù xīng)

中国历史（下）

17.
huàn guān	huáng qīn guó qì	cái fù	chǔ jìng	zhuàng dà	cōngmáng	shōu fù
宦官	皇親國戚	財富	處境	壯大	匆忙	收復

xià mén	qū zhú	hé lán	jī dì	jiā shǔ	zhānghuà	zhì lǐ	guī shùn
廈門	驅逐	荷蘭	基地	家屬	彰化	治理	歸順

18.
chéng jī	kāng xī	qiān dìng	huà dìng	qián lóng	zhǔn gá ěr	fù dān
乘機	康熙	簽訂	劃定	乾隆	準噶爾	負擔

rì ěr màn	jì kǒng	chù jí	zì jū	jué chá	mín zhǔ	qì yuē	zhuān zhì
日耳曼	祭孔	觸及	自居	覺察	民主	契約	專制

yǐ zhì	cháo liú
（以）致	潮流

19.
nì chā	ní róng	jù jué	zuì è	yā piàn	shōu jiǎo	xiāo huǐ	jūn jiàn
逆差	呢絨	拒絕	罪惡	鴉片	收繳	銷毀	軍艦

péi cháng	cái pàn	zhí mín dì	wán gù	tán	xīn hài gé mìng	xiǎng yìng
賠償	裁判	殖民地	頑固	譚	辛亥革命	響應

lín shí	kǎi
臨時	凱

共計 139 個生詞

中国历史朝代年表

夏　约公元前 21 世纪——约公元前 17 世纪

商　约公元前 17 世纪——约公元前 11 世纪

周　西周　约公元前 11 世纪——公元前 771 年

　　东周　公元前 770 年——公元前 256 年

　　　春秋时代　公元前 770 年——公元前 476 年

　　　战国时代　公元前 475 年——公元前 221 年

秦　公元前 221 年——公元前 206 年

汉　西汉　公元前 206 年——公元 25 年

　　东汉　公元 25 年——公元 220 年

三国（魏蜀吴）公元 220 年——公元 280 年

西晋　公元 265 年——公元 317 年

东晋　十六国　公元 317 年——公元 420 年

南北朝　公元 420 年——公元 589 年

隋		公元 581 年——公元 618 年
唐		公元 618 年——公元 907 年
五代十国		公元 907 年——公元 960 年
宋	北宋	公元 960 年——公元 1127 年
	南宋	公元 1127 年——公元 1279 年
辽		公元 916 年——公元 1125 年
西夏		公元 1038 年——公元 1227 年
金		公元 1115 年——公元 1234 年
元		公元 1271 年——公元 1368 年
明		公元 1368 年——公元 1644 年
清		公元 1644 年——公元 1911 年

第十一课

一 写生词

蓬	勃										
富	庶										
宠	爱										
贵	妃										
无	奈										
黄	巢										
叛	变										
灿	烂										
允	许										
欧	阳	询									

二 组词

蓬_____ 腐_____ 奈_____ 宗_____

灿_____ 叛_____ 庶_____ 妃_____

宠_____ 爆_____ 播_____ 愤_____

三 选字组词

无(奈 耐)　　(允 充)许　　蓬(脖 勃)

(奈 耐)心　　(允 充)分　　(脖 勃)子

四 根据课文选择正确答案

1. 唐朝前期,唐是当时世界上最_____。

　　A 衰弱落后的国家　　B 富庶、强盛的国家

2. 安史之乱以后,唐朝走向_____。

　　A 衰落　　B 蓬勃发展

3. 唐朝末年爆发了_____起义,唐帝国灭亡。

　　A 黄巾　　B 黄巢

4. 隋唐时期,与中国通商的国家有_____个。

　　A 17　　B 70 多

5. 在长安、洛阳、广州等城市,有来自新罗(朝鲜)_____等国的外国商人和留学生。

  A 日本、波斯和东罗马 B 波斯、非洲、美洲

6. 唐朝政府平等对待外国人,允许他们在中国居住,和中国人_____。

  A 通婚   B 当官

7. 在长安、洛阳这些大城市,有许多外国商人开的_____。

  A 商店和酒馆   B 街道和图书馆

8. 在_____时期,景教、伊斯兰教也传入了中国。

  A 秦汉   B 隋唐   C 春秋战国

9. 唐朝是中国诗歌的黄金时代,著名诗人有_____。

  A 李白和唐僧等   B 李白、杜甫和白居易等

10. 唐玄宗时,天文学家_____测量出了子午线的长度。

  A 一行和尚   B 一行教授

五 造句

1. 无奈_____

2. 允许_____

六 回答问题

1. 唐朝是中国历史上很开放的时期,对吗?请举例说一说当时开放的情况。

答:＿＿＿＿＿＿＿＿＿＿＿＿＿＿＿＿＿＿＿＿＿＿

＿＿＿＿＿＿＿＿＿＿＿＿＿＿＿＿＿＿＿＿＿＿＿＿

2. 唐代有多少国家和中国通商?

答:＿＿＿＿＿＿＿＿＿＿＿＿＿＿＿＿＿＿＿＿＿＿

＿＿＿＿＿＿＿＿＿＿＿＿＿＿＿＿＿＿＿＿＿＿＿＿

3. 隋唐时期有哪些著名的建筑?

答:＿＿＿＿＿＿＿＿＿＿＿＿＿＿＿＿＿＿＿＿＿＿

＿＿＿＿＿＿＿＿＿＿＿＿＿＿＿＿＿＿＿＿＿＿＿＿

4. 唐代汉族和其他民族生活在一起,对文化的发展有什么好处?

答:＿＿＿＿＿＿＿＿＿＿＿＿＿＿＿＿＿＿＿＿＿＿

＿＿＿＿＿＿＿＿＿＿＿＿＿＿＿＿＿＿＿＿＿＿＿＿

七 根据阅读材料选择填空

1. 莫高窟,俗称千佛洞,位于_____省。

(河北　甘肃)

2. 公元366年,一位_____在崖(yá)壁上建造了第一个佛窟。

(僧人　艺术家)

3. 敦煌(dūn huáng)莫高窟壁画有许多_____故事。

(伊(yī)斯兰教　佛教)

4. "飞天"和"反弹琵琶(pí bā)"等是敦煌_____的代表作。

(壁画　塑像)

5. 莫高窟是一座_____的宝库。

(文化艺术　科学技术)

八 写一写《灿烂的隋唐文化》(不少于200字)

_____

_____

_____

九 熟读课文

第十三课

一　写生词

契	丹										
党	项										
俘	虏										
召	回										
文	天	祥									
侵	略										
钞	票										
千	古	流	芳								

二 组词

境_____　　维_____　　制_____　　谋_____

应_____　　伐_____　　钞_____　　俘_____

侵_____　　芳_____

三 选字组词

（芳　方）香　　边（境　镜）　　维（持　特）

（芳　方）向　　（境　镜）子　　（持　特）别

（钞　吵）票　　文天（祥　详）

争（钞　吵）　　（祥　详）细

四 根据课文选择正确答案

1. 宋朝当时有三个敌人：_____。

（战国　辽国　西夏　金国）

2. 辽是_____建立的。（契丹人　女真族）

3. 金国是_____建立的。（女真族　契丹人）

4. 宋徽宗的另一个儿子于公元1127年在临安建立_____。　　　　　　　　　　　　　　　（南宋　唐朝）

5. 岳飞是宋朝著名的_____将领。（抗金　抗日）

6. 忽必烈于公元1271年建立_____。（汉朝　元朝）

7. _____写下了"人生自古谁无死,留取丹心照汗青"的诗句。　　　　　　　　　　　　　（文天祥　岳飞）

8. 宋朝的_____在当时世界上是非常先进的。

　　　　　　　　　　　（建筑业　陶瓷业和造船业）

9. 宋朝出现了世界上最早的_____——交子。

　　　　　　　　　　　　　　　　（金币　纸币）

10. 活字印刷是_____时发明的。

　　　　　　　　　　　　　（汉朝　秦朝　宋朝）

11. 发明于唐代的火药到宋代_____。

　　　　　　　　　　　（已广泛应用　未广泛应用）

五　造句

1. 顺利_____

2. 应用_____

六 回答问题

1. 契丹人和西夏人怎样学习汉文化?

答:_____

_____

_____

2. 契丹、党项等民族学习汉文化对民族融合有什么好处?(选做题)

答:_____

_____

七 根根据阅读材料选择填空

1. 岳飞的军队叫"岳家军",金军十分_____他们。

(害怕 勇敢)

2. 岳飞热爱祖国,被称为_____。(英雄 将军)

3. 秦桧杀害岳飞,_____被人唾骂。(世代 年代)
   （huì）   （tuò）

八 写一写《发达的两宋文化》(不少于200字)

九 熟读课文

第十五课

一 写生词

检	查										
开	垦										
桑											
提	倡										
活	跃										
漕	运										
制	订										
窦											
西	厢	记									
歧	视										
赫	赫	武	功								

澎	湖	列	岛								

二 组词

跃_____　　倡_____　　垦_____　　厢_____

检_____　　歧_____　　领_____　　等_____

三 选字组词

(跃　妖)精　　　激(烈　列)　　　(歧　枝)视

活(跃　妖)　　　排(烈　列)　　　树(歧　枝)

检(起　查)　　　提(昌　倡)　　　车(厢　相)

捡(起　查)　　　许(昌　倡)　　　(厢　相)信

四 写出近义词

开端——　　　　　　以往——

五 根据课文选择正确答案

1. 忽必烈建立的元朝是_____的王朝。

   A 蒙古族　　　　B 藏族　　　　C 汉族

2. 忽必烈是一位杰出的皇帝,他保护农业,大力_____。

   A 推行汉法　　　　B 推广蒙古文化

3. 忽必烈提倡以_____为主的汉族传统文化。

   A 儒学　　　　B 天主教　　　　C 道家

4. 元朝为了保住蒙古贵族的地位,实行_____的政策。

   A 民族歧视　　　　　　B 民族平等

5. 元朝中期,海外贸易空前发达,有许多外国商人和使节_____居住在北京。

   A 长期　　　　　　B 短期

6. 郭守敬是元朝著名的_____。

   A 文学家　　　　　　B 天文学家

7. 元朝的黄道婆改进了当时的_____技术。

   A 棉纺织　　　　B 造纸　　　　C 制茶

8. 元代文化最著名的是_____，它是现代戏曲的开端。

　　A 唐诗　　　　　B 宋词　　　　　C 元曲

六　造句

　　激烈 _____

七　词语解释

　　1. 空前——
　　2. 见闻——

八　回答问题

　　1. 忽必烈为什么要重用汉人？
　　答：_____
　　_____

　　2. 忽必烈怎样推行汉法？
　　答：_____
　　_____

九 根据阅读材料选择填空

1. 马可·波罗是_____人。（意大利　英国）

2. 马可·波罗是第一个将中国介绍给_____的人。
（美洲　欧洲）

3. 马可·波罗和父亲、叔(shū)父三人一路历经_____来到中国。　　　　（轻松愉快　千辛万苦）

4. 忽必烈很_____马可·波罗，派他到国内各地和邻近国家进行访问。　　　　（依靠　信任）

5. 马可·波罗和父亲、叔父在中国生活了_____年。他们想回家乡威尼斯看看。　　　　(17　7)

6. 马可·波罗在监狱中把关于_____的故事讲给一位作家听，这位作家写出了著名的《马可·波罗游记》。　　　　（中国　美国）

十　任选下列一个题目写一篇短文（不少于200字）

　　1.《元世祖忽必烈》

　　2.《马可·波罗的故事》

十一　熟读课文

第十七课

一 写生词

宦	官										
匆	忙										
厦	门										
彰	化										

二 组词

宦_____   戚_____   厦_____   降_____

属_____   驱_____   荷_____   奖_____

顺_____   壮_____   复_____   富_____

匆_____   财_____   基_____

三 选字组词

亲（戚 成）　　　白（免 兔）　　　奖（历 励）
（戚 成）功　　　（免 兔）去　　　（历 励）史

（驱 区）逐　　　（厦 夏）门　　　（匆 勿）忙
（驱 区）别　　　（厦 夏）天　　　请（匆 勿）吸烟

四 写出近义词

收复——　　　　　投降——　　　　　宦官——

五 根据课文选择填空

1. 公元1661年郑成功带领2.5万名_____和几百艘战船，向台湾进军。　　　　　（将士　农民）

2. 郑成功收复台湾后，下令让几万士兵和随军家属_____。　　　　　（练兵　开荒种田）

3. 郑成功祖孙三代治理台湾_____年。（22　40）

4. 郑氏三代的治理在台湾历史上是一个重要的开发和发展时期，称为"_____"。　　（明郑时代　明清时代）

六 根据课文选择正确答案

1. 明朝中后期,宦官专权,政治_____,皇亲国戚占有大量土地和财富。

　　A 开放　　　　　B 腐败

2. 明末农民起义军的领袖_____带领起义军攻入北京,明朝灭亡。

　　A 郑成功　　　　B 李自成

3. 明朝大将吴三桂投降_____,联合清军一起攻打起义军。

　　A 清　　　　　　B 宋

4. 清军占领北京,并把首都迁到_____,开始了对全国的统治。

　　A 北京　　　　　B 天津

5. 郑成功是抗清名将,也是收复_____的民族英雄。

　　A 台湾　　　　　B 河北

6. 公元 1662 年,郑成功驱逐了_____,收回了台湾,以台湾为抗清的基地。

　　A 西班牙人　　　B 荷兰人　　　C 英国人

7. 公元1683年,清政府派军进攻台湾,郑克塽(shuǎng)归顺。自此台湾在清政府直接统治下,属_____省。

　　A 福建　　　　　B 广东

七　回答问题

　　1. 郑成功对台湾有什么贡献?

　　答:_____

　　_____

　　2. 根据阅读材料谈一谈为什么利玛窦(mǎ)得到了中国人的信任和友谊(yì)。

　　答:_____

　　_____

　　_____

八　根据阅读材料选择填空

　　1. 16世纪,一些欧洲天主教教士来中国_____,其中最有名的是利玛窦。　　　　　(传教　经商　打仗)

2. 利玛窦是_____人,耶稣会教士。1582年到中国传教。他建立了中国内地的第一座天主教堂。

(意大利 德国)

3. 利玛窦努力学习汉语,精通"四书五经",_____中国文化,得到了中国人的信任和友谊。(尊重 喜欢)

4. 利玛窦还将西方的_____、三角学、西方乐器等介绍给中国人。 (佛学 几何学)

5. 利玛窦把中国经典"四书"、"五经"、《道德经》等译成拉丁文,介绍到欧洲,成为第一个把_____介绍给西方的人。 (孔子和儒家思想 孙子兵法)

九 任选下列一个题目写一篇短文(不少于200字)

1.《民族英雄郑成功》

2.《利玛窦的故事》

十 熟读课文

第十九课

一 写生词

逆	差										
呢	绒										
拒	绝										
收	缴										
军	舰										
赔	偿										
裁	判										
谭											
凯											
辛	亥	革	命								

二 组词

凯_____ 绝_____ 鸦_____ 舰_____

顽_____ 偿_____ 罪_____ 殖_____

三 选字组词

(赔 倍)款　　军(舰 船)　　(顽 玩)固

一(赔 倍)　　木(舰 船)　　(顽 玩)具

(殖 值)民地　　(裁 栽)判　　赔(尝 偿)

价(殖 值)　　(裁 栽)种　　(尝 偿)试

四 写出反义词

逆差——　　　　　　拒绝——

五 根据课文选择正确答案

1. 18世纪末，英国从中国进口大量茶叶，在中英贸易中，英国一直有很大的_____。

   A 逆差　　　　B 顺差

2. 英国想以外交手段打开中国市场，但是被乾隆皇帝_____了。

    A 同意　　　　　B 拒绝

3. 为了改变贸易逆差，英国居然开始了罪恶的_____贸易。

    A 鸦片　　　　　B 茶叶　　　　　C 瓷器

4. 到了1838年，每年有_____鸦片卖到中国。

    A 四百多箱　　　B 四千多箱　　　C 四万多箱

5. 清朝皇帝命令林则徐禁烟。林则徐在虎门将收缴的鸦片全部销毁，这就是历史上著名的"_____"。

    A 鸦片战争　　　B 虎门销烟

6. 1840年，英国派军舰入侵中国，发动了"_____"。

    A 中法战争　　　B 鸦片战争

7. 1842年，清政府被迫同英国签订了中国近代史上第一个_____——《南京条约》。

    A 不平等条约　　B 平等条约

8. 签订《南京条约》以后的中国沦为_____社会。

    A 殖民地　　　　B 半殖民地半封建

9. 1911年，_____领导的辛亥革命推翻了清帝国。

    A 林则徐　　　　B 孙中山

10. 辛亥革命推翻了_____王朝,建立了中华民国。

    A 明   B 清

六 造句

1. 忍受_____

2. 拒绝_____

七 词语解释

1. 冒天下之大不韪(wěi)——

2. 举世无双——

八 回答问题

1. 鸦片战争爆发的原因是什么?

答:_____

_____

_____

2.为什么说签订《南京条约》使中国变为半殖民地半封建的国家？

答：_____

_____

_____

3.什么革命推翻了清朝？革命的领导人是谁？

答：_____

_____

九 根据阅读材料判断对错

1. 清朝皇帝派林则徐去广西禁烟。　　　　____对　____错

2. 林则徐下令限外商5天内交出所有鸦片。　　　　　　　　　　　　　____对　____错

3. 林则徐还下令外商个人出保证书，声明：以后来船绝不夹带鸦片。　　　　____对　____错

4. 林则徐又在广东省内，下令严禁贩卖、吸食鸦片。　　　　　　　　　　____对　____错

5. 两个月内，林则徐收缴外商鸦片2万多箱。　　　　　　　　　　　　____对　____错

十　写一写《鸦片战争和南京条约》(不少于200字)

十一　熟读课文

第十一课听写

第十三课听写

第十五课听写

第十二课

一 写生词

财	政										

昏	庸										

奸	臣										

宋	钦	宗									

掳	走										

瑰	宝										

不	朽										

二 组词

宴_____ 纳_____ 财_____ 贷_____

割_____ 赔_____ 瑰_____ 朽_____

罢_____ 革_____ 利_____

三 选字组词

（割　害）草　　　棉（币　布）

（割　害）怕　　　钱（币　布）

四 根据课文选择正确答案

1. 唐朝灭亡后,中国又分裂成很多小国,历史上把这一时期总称为"_____"。

   A 五代十国　　　　B 十国

2. 公元960年,赵匡kuāng yìn胤建立_____,史称北宋。

   A 宋朝　　　　B 汉朝　　　　C 唐朝

3. _____王安石在皇帝的支持下开始变法。

   A 将军　　　　B 改革家　　　　C 太子

4. 王安石推行新法,最后_____。

   A 失败了　　　　B 成功了

5. 北宋被_____灭亡。

   A 辽国　　　　B 金国　　　　C 西夏

6. 北宋时,虽然战乱不断,但南方比较_____。

   A 安静　　　　B 安宁　　　　C 安心

7. 北宋时，_____有明显的进步。

    A 文学艺术　　　　B 军事　　　　C 科学技术

五　造句

结束_____

六　回答问题

1. 王安石变法的主要内容是什么？

答：_____

_____

2. "万般皆下品，唯有读书高"的观念和科举制度有没有关系？

答：_____

_____

七　根据阅读材料选择填空

1. 北宋时，_____发达，宋是当时世界上的商业大国。

（商业　艺术）

2. 宋朝，在一些港口和交通要道出现了许多_____。

（乡村　城镇）

3. 北宋的都城有居民_____户。　（20万　10万）

4. 北宋都城内_____有数不清的店铺、酒楼、饭馆。

（大街小巷　广场）

5. 北宋都城还有娱乐场所，那里有戏曲、杂技和_____表演。　　　　　　　　　　（武术　电影）

6.《清明上河图》是宋朝画家_____的作品。

（张择端　李白）

7.《清明上河图》画的是汴京_____的情景。

（真实生活　神仙）

八　根据阅读材料选词填空（把词语写在空白处）

人口　　城镇　　商业　　情景　　画卷　　生活

繁华的_____　　发达的_____　　流动的_____

真实的_____　　长长的_____　　热闹的_____

九 写一写《清明上河图》(不少于200字)

十 熟读课文

第十四课

一 写生词

奔	驰											
匈	牙	利										
旭	烈	兀										
跨												
莱	茵	河										
伊	朗											
伊	拉	克										
缅	甸											

二 组词

牧_____　　尚_____　　混_____　　率_____

征_____　　续_____　　驰_____　　匈_____

机_____　　滨_____　　占_____　　括_____

三 选字组词

(匈　胸)牙利　　　　(跨　夸)越　　　　缅(句　甸)

(匈　胸)有成竹　　　(跨　夸)奖　　　　(句　甸)子

(占　站)领　　　　　土(耳　而)其

(占　站)立　　　　　(耳　而)且

四 根据课文选择正确答案

1. 蒙古族是生活在蒙古草原上的_____民族。

　　A 游牧　　　　　B 农业　　　　　C 商业

2. 成吉思汗的名字是_____。

　　A 忽必烈　　　　B 铁木真

3. 成吉思汗和他的子孙建立了_____的蒙古大帝国。

　　A 黄河流域　　　B 地跨欧亚　　　C 欧洲

4. 成吉思汗的孙子忽必烈建立了_____,他就是元世祖。

　　A 元朝　　　　　B 宋朝

5. 元朝的首都是今天的_____。

　　A 南京　　　　　B 北京　　　　　C 上海

五 造句

本领_____

六 词语解释

1. 尚武——
2. 吃苦——
3. 绝好——

七 回答问题

1. 蒙古强大起来的原因是什么？

答：_____
_____
_____
_____

2. 根据阅读材料简述中西交通的历史。

答：_____
_____
_____

八 根据阅读材料判断对错

1. 中国对外交通,开始于汉代的丝绸之路。

　　　　　　　　　　　　　　　　___对　___错

2. 隋唐时期,对外交通除了陆路还有海路。

　　　　　　　　　　　　　　　　___对　___错

3. 宋代陆路交通中断,但海路贸易繁荣。　___对　___错

4. 元帝国横跨欧亚,使"世界"大通。　　___对　___错

5. 元代,东西文化互相传播。　　　　　　___对　___错

6. 元政府在长一万多里的交通大道上建了很多驿站。

　　　　　　　　　　　　　　　　___对　___错

7. 元朝,海运事业特别发达。　　　　　　___对　___错

九 写一写《元代的中西交通》(不少于200字)

_____

_____

_____

_____

_____

十 熟读课文

第十六课

一 写生词

郑	成	功									
嘉	峪	关									
雇	佣										
窑											
销	售										
徐	光	启									
采	煤										
金	碧	辉	煌								

二 组词

启_____　　销_____　　镇_____　　煤_____

雇_____　　途_____　　余_____　　碧_____

三 选字组词

（启　起）发　　　（销　消）售　　　金(壁　碧)辉煌

（启　起）来　　　（销　消）息　　　墙(壁　碧)

四 根据课文选择填空

1. 明朝手工业和商业发达，丝绸和_____十分精美。

（青花瓷　棉布）

2. 中国瓷器和丝绸出口到欧洲和美洲，换取了大量的_____。

（黄金　白银）

3. 《本草纲目》是一部药物学巨著，是当时世界上内容最丰富、最详细的药物学_____。　　（文献　字典）

4. 《农政全书》是徐光启写的一部_____百科全书。

（农业　工业）

5. 徐光启和意大利传教士利玛(mǎ)窦翻译了中国历史上第一部科技译著_____。　　（《圣经》　《几何原本》）

6. 《天工开物》是_____编写的。　（宋应星　徐光启）

7.《天工开物》被称为"中国17世纪的_____"。

（古典小说　诗词　工艺百科全书）

8.著名的长篇小说《三国演义》、《水浒(hǔ)传》和《西游记》等都写于_____。　　　　（宋代　明代　唐代）

五 根据课文选择正确答案

1.公元1402年,燕(yān)王朱棣赶走建文帝(dì),自己做了皇帝,并把首都迁到了_____。

A 上海　　　　B 北京　　　　C 天津

2.北京成为明朝的首都以后,一直是中国_____的中心。

A 商业　　　　B 政治、经济和文化　　　　C 艺术

3.北京的皇宫金碧辉煌,是现今世界上_____古代宫殿建筑群。

A 最美丽的　　　　B 最大、保留最完整的

4.明朝前期是一个繁荣开放的国家。明朝中后期中国开始_____。

A 衰落　　　　B 发达

六 造句

1. 多余_____

2. 沿途_____

七 词语解释

1. 金碧辉煌——

2. 胸怀大志——

八 回答问题

明朝的科学家写出的三部科学巨著是哪三部书？

答：_____

_____

九 根据阅读材料选择填空

1. 明成祖是一位思想比较_____的皇帝，他派太监郑和率船队出使西洋。　　　　（开放　开朗　封闭）

2. 公元1405年农历六月的一天，郑和带领_____扬帆南下。　　　　　　　　　　　（船队　商队）

3. 明朝前期,中国的纺织、制瓷、造船、航海业都处在世界_____地位。　　　　　　　　　　（落后　领先）

4. 郑和原来姓马,_____人。公元1371年出生在云南。　　　　　　　　　　　　　　　（汉族　回族）

5. 郑和第一次下西洋,他的船队共有_____人,有水手、官兵、工匠、医生、翻译等。船队之大,是当时世界上独一无二的。　　　　　　　　　（2.7万　5,000）

6. 郑和的宝船长约138米,宽56米,可容纳_____人,是当时世界上最大的海船。　　（1,000　500　100）

7. 郑和七次下西洋,他的船队到过亚洲和非洲的_____多个国家和地区。　　　　　　（30　20）

十　任选下列一个题目写一篇短文(不少于200字)

1.《明朝的瓷器和丝绸的生产情况》

2.《郑和下西洋》

_____

_____

_____

_____

十一 熟读课文

第十八课

一 写生词

康	熙											
乾	隆											
准	噶	尔										
日	耳	曼										
祭	孔											
以	致											

二 组词

负_____   居_____   察_____   证_____

倡_____   签_____   致_____   乘_____

曼_____   潮_____   触_____   徒_____

三 选字组词

（担 但）是　　　（提 题）目　　　觉（查 察）

负（担 但）　　　（提 题）倡　　　检（查 察）

（定 订）婚　　　奖（厉 励）　　　（潮 朝）流

决（定 订）　　　（厉 励）害　　　（潮 朝）鲜

四 根据课文选择正确答案

1. 清朝是中国封建社会最后一个朝代，是由_____建立的。

   A 蒙古族　　　B 满族　　　C 汉族

2. 康熙皇帝于公元1683年出兵统一了_____。

   A 海南　　　B 台湾

3. 乾隆皇帝注意发展边疆经济文化，巩固了中国_____国家的统一。

   A 多民族　　　B 单一民族

4. 从康熙到乾隆三朝，国家稳定，社会繁荣，被称为"_____"。

   A 大唐盛世　　　　B 康乾盛世

5. 清王朝盲目自大，并未觉察欧洲正发生着_____的变化。

   A 翻天覆地　　　　B 反反复复

6. 早在1582年，意大利传教士利玛窦等已来到中国_____。

   A 传教　　　　　　B 经商

7. 传教士来到中国，带来了西方的科学知识。同时，他们也学习中国的_____。

   A 儒学、佛学　　　B 祭孔祭祖

8. 法国、美国建立了民主政权，人民用_____治理自己的国家。

   A 彩票　　　　　　B 选票

9. 大清国文化上提封建礼教，大兴_____。

   A 文字狱　　　　　B 监狱

10. 清政府闭关自守，使中国远远_____于世界的先进潮流。

    A 落后　　　　　　B 赶上

五 造句

1. 自大＿＿＿＿＿＿＿＿＿＿＿＿＿＿＿＿＿

2. 乘机＿＿＿＿＿＿＿＿＿＿＿＿＿＿＿＿＿

六 回答问题

1. "康乾盛世"的同一时期，欧洲发生了什么变化？

答：＿＿＿＿＿＿＿＿＿＿＿＿＿＿＿＿＿＿

＿＿＿＿＿＿＿＿＿＿＿＿＿＿＿＿＿＿＿＿

＿＿＿＿＿＿＿＿＿＿＿＿＿＿＿＿＿＿＿＿

＿＿＿＿＿＿＿＿＿＿＿＿＿＿＿＿＿＿＿＿

2. 清政府觉察到欧洲的巨大变化了吗？它采取了什么样的做法？造成了什么样的后果？

答：＿＿＿＿＿＿＿＿＿＿＿＿＿＿＿＿＿＿

＿＿＿＿＿＿＿＿＿＿＿＿＿＿＿＿＿＿＿＿

＿＿＿＿＿＿＿＿＿＿＿＿＿＿＿＿＿＿＿＿

＿＿＿＿＿＿＿＿＿＿＿＿＿＿＿＿＿＿＿＿

七 根据阅读材料选择填空

1. 清朝的文化思想，_____儒家礼教，打压反清言行和文字。（提倡 打压）

2. 康乾时期，由官方组织大批_____编写了《四库全书》和《康熙字典》等许多书籍。（学者 医生）

3. 《四库全书》由乾隆皇帝亲自主持，是封建社会_____修订的最大丛书。（民间 官方）

4. 《四库全书》编成后，抄成七份，分别藏于北京故宫和江浙等地的藏书楼中。其中江浙藏书楼对公众开放，供各地文人_____。（买卖 查阅）

八 写一写《清朝落后于欧美国家的原因》（不少于200字）

九 熟读课文

第十二课听写

第十四课听写

第十六课听写

中国历史(下)

第十八课听写

练习纸

中国历史(下)

练习纸

中国历史(下)